Colorful Flower Garden

Put flower stickers wherever you'd like in the garden.
Then, add butterfly and ladybug stickers.

T0060086

Beach Day

Give the kids beach toy stickers. Then, add sea creature stickers on the beach.

example

Sticker

Good job!

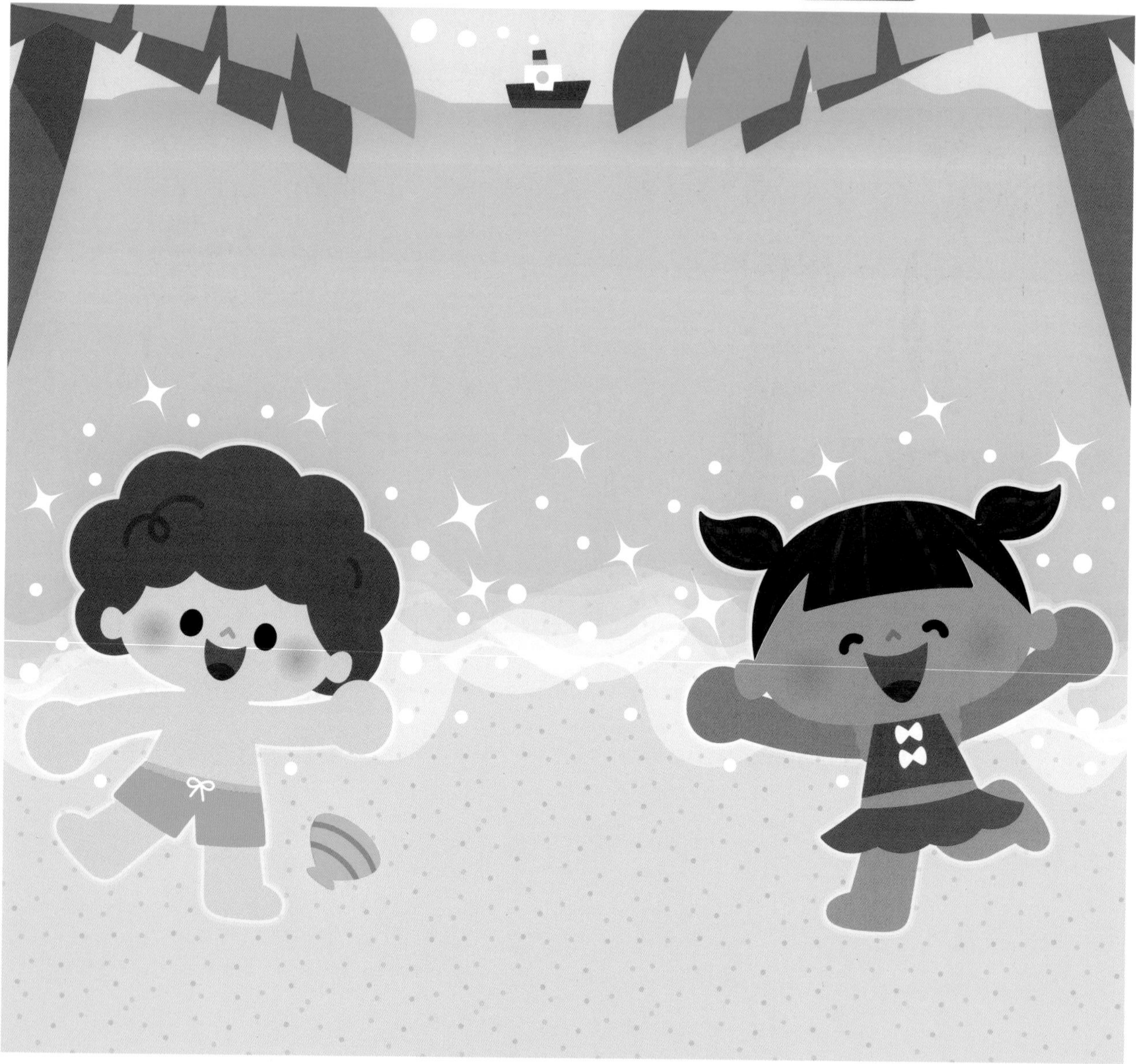

Creativity

Make a Pattern on the Cow

Put stickers on the cow to create a pattern.

example

Sticker
Good job!

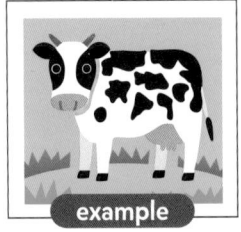

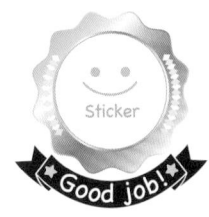

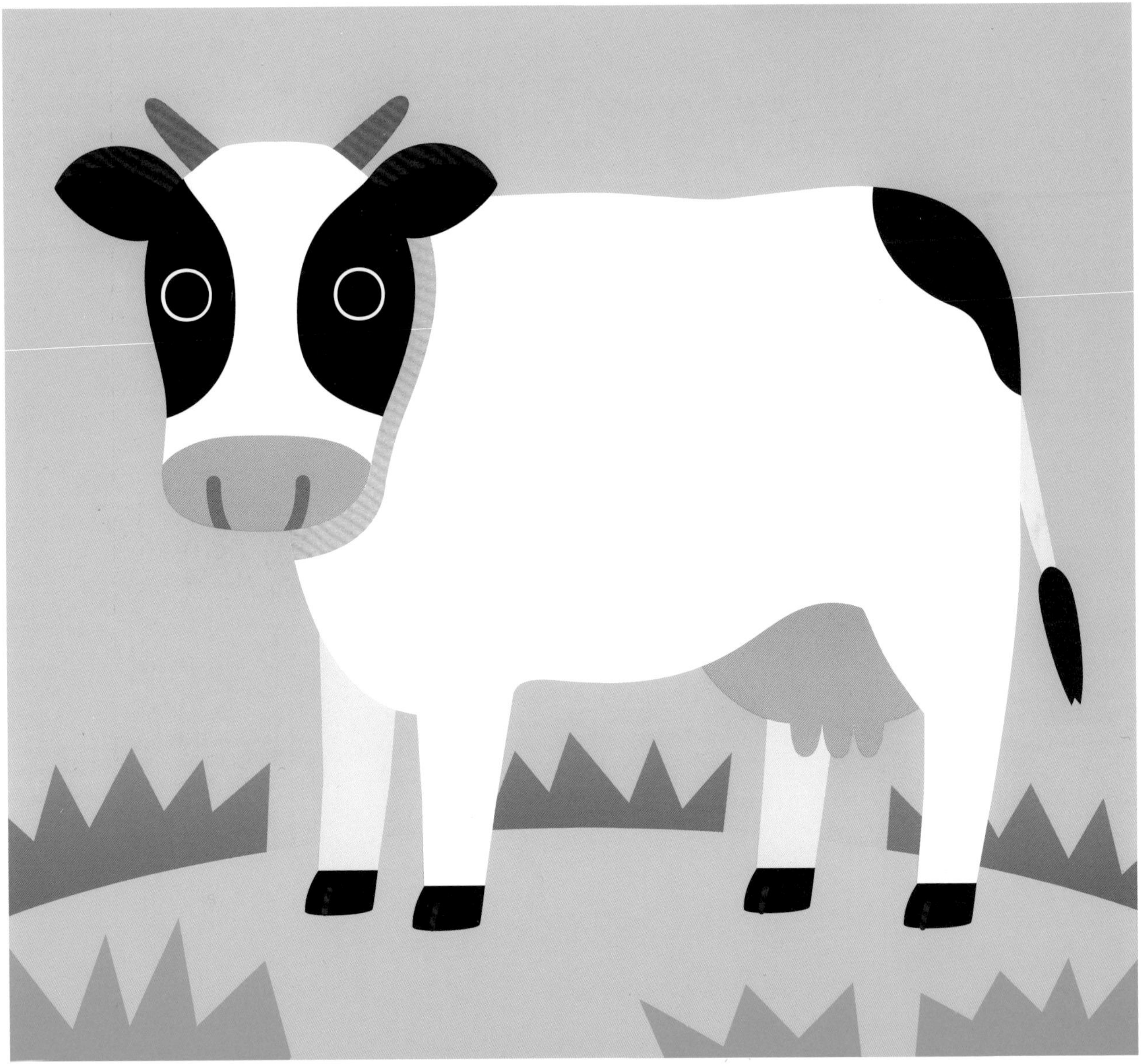

Puppy Play

Put each dog sticker on its matching shadow. Then, find toy stickers and give them to the dogs.

Sticker

Good job!

Yummy Fruit

What fruit do you see? Put each fruit sticker on its matching shadow.

Sticker

Good job!

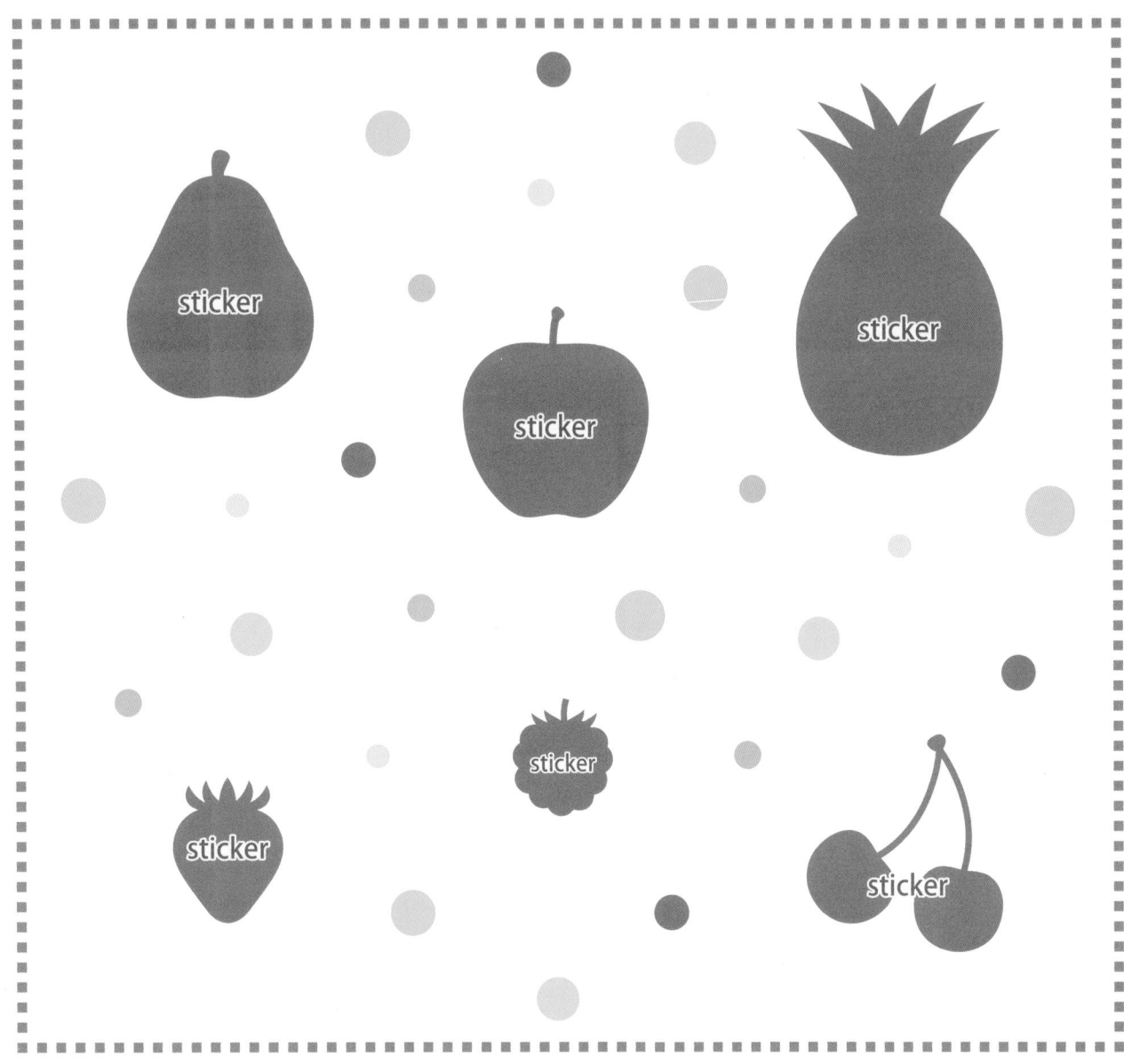

Match the Shadows

Find the stickers that match the shadows. Then, put one sticker in each box.

Sticker
★ Good job! ★

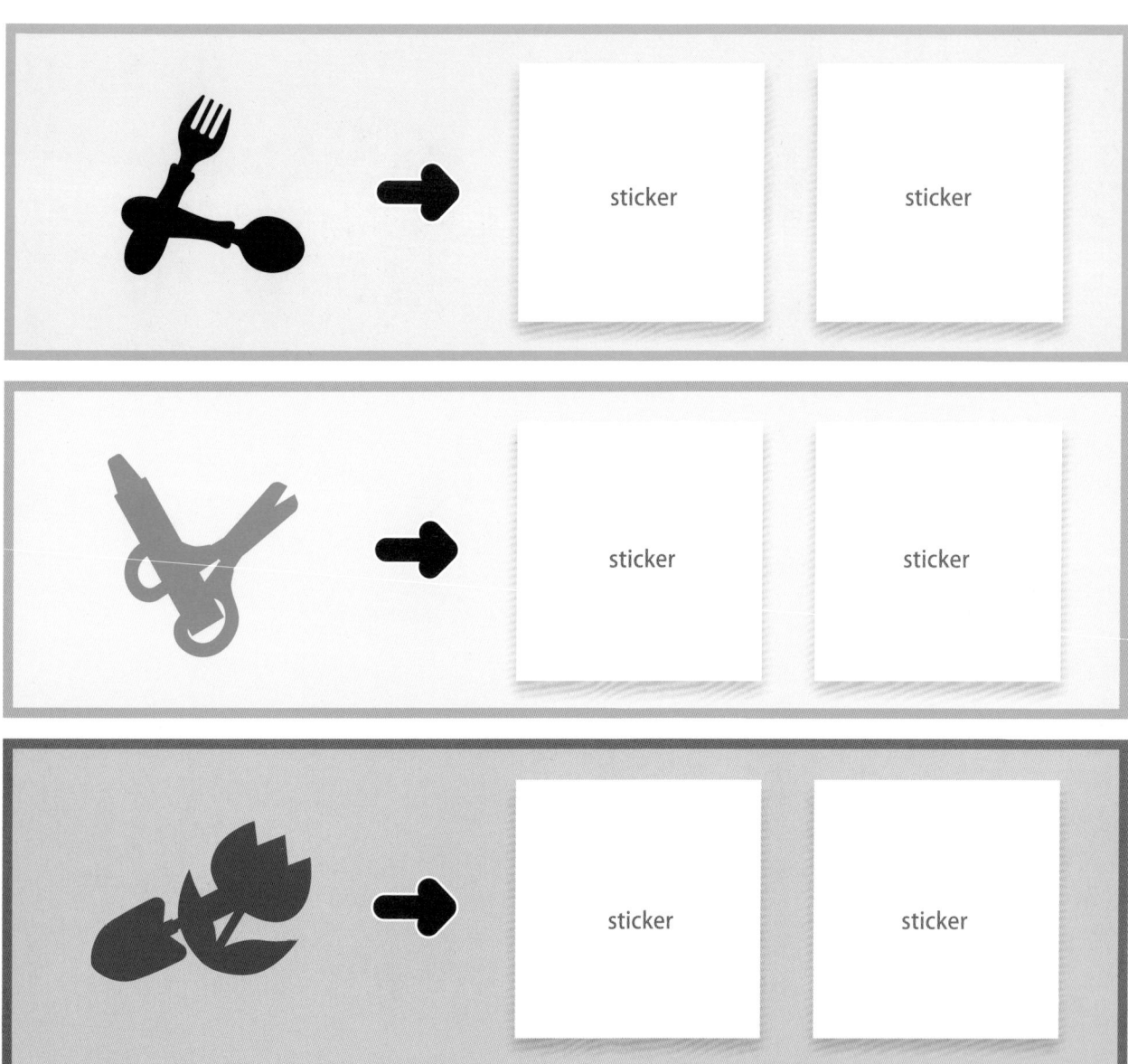

sticker sticker

sticker sticker

sticker sticker

Picture Puzzle

Animal Game

Put stickers on the pig and rabbit to complete the pictures.

Sticker
Good job!

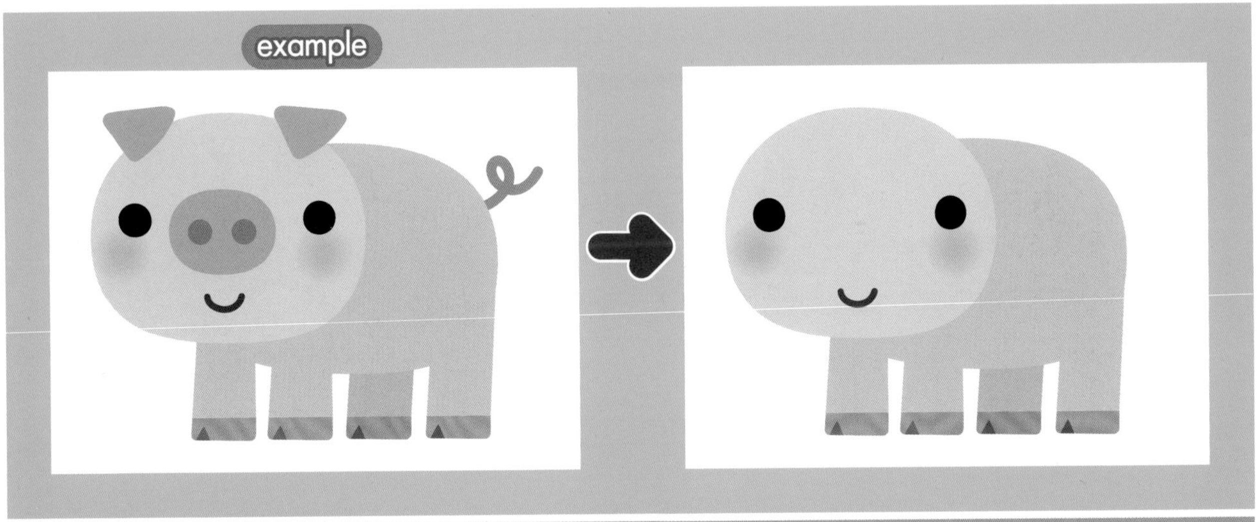
example

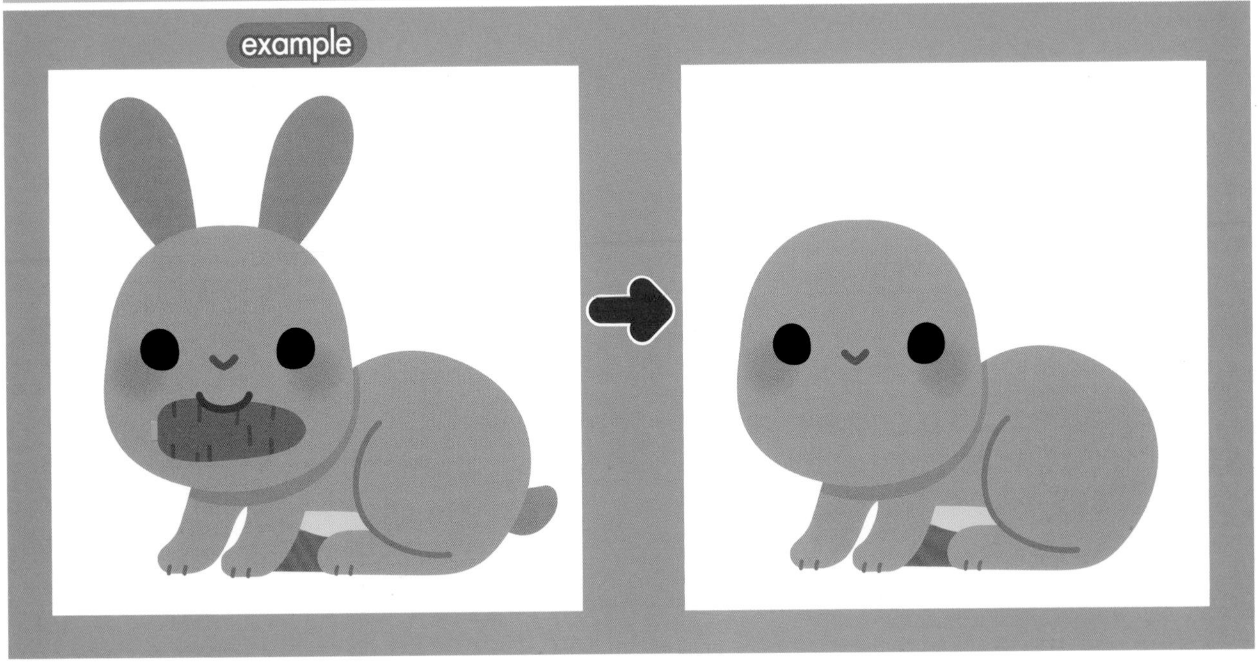
example

Picture Match

Add vegetable stickers to the bottom plate so it matches the top plate.

Sticker
Good job!

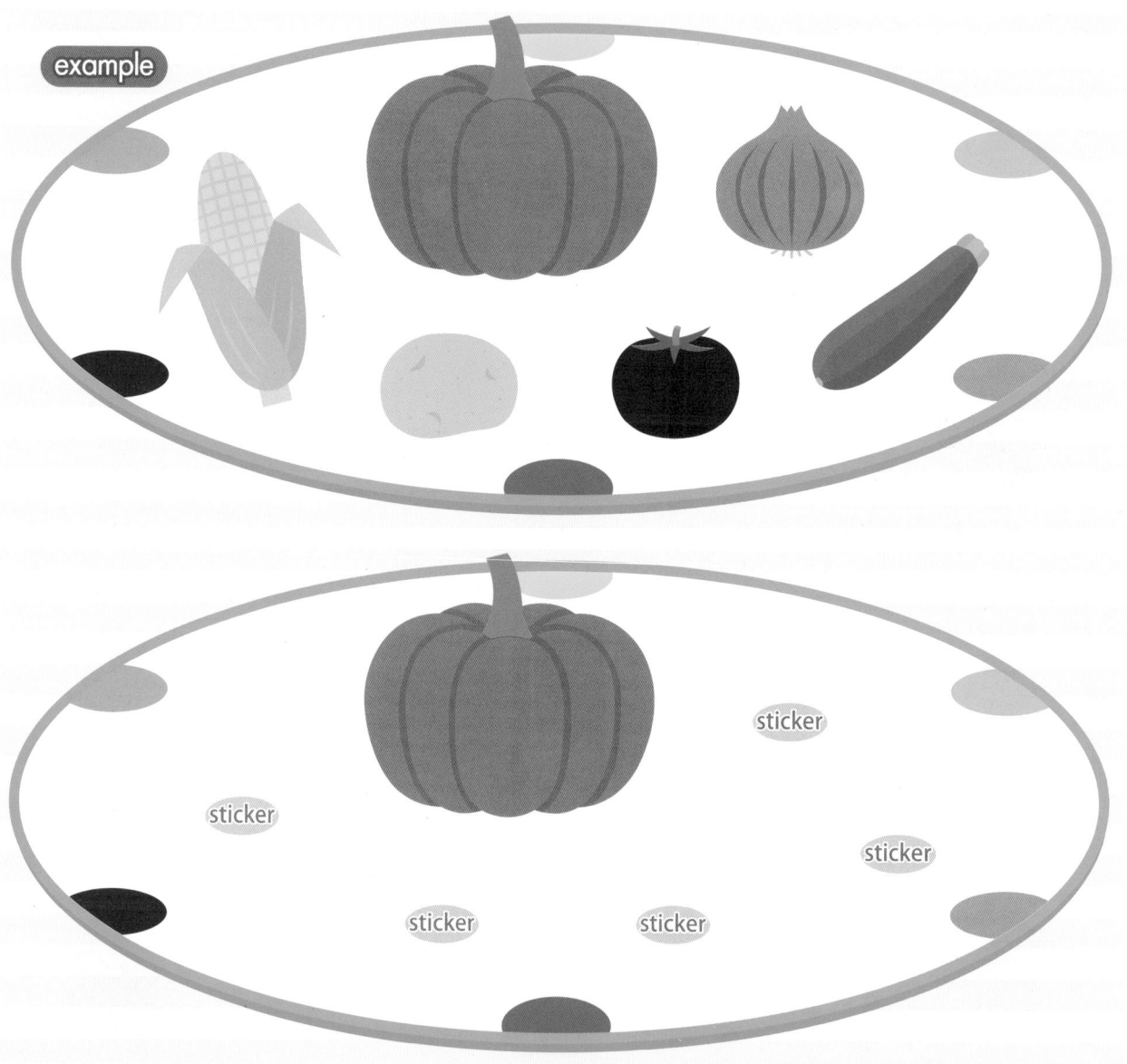

example

sticker

sticker

sticker

sticker

sticker

Picture Match

Put animal stickers on the right so it matches the scene on the left.

Good job!

example

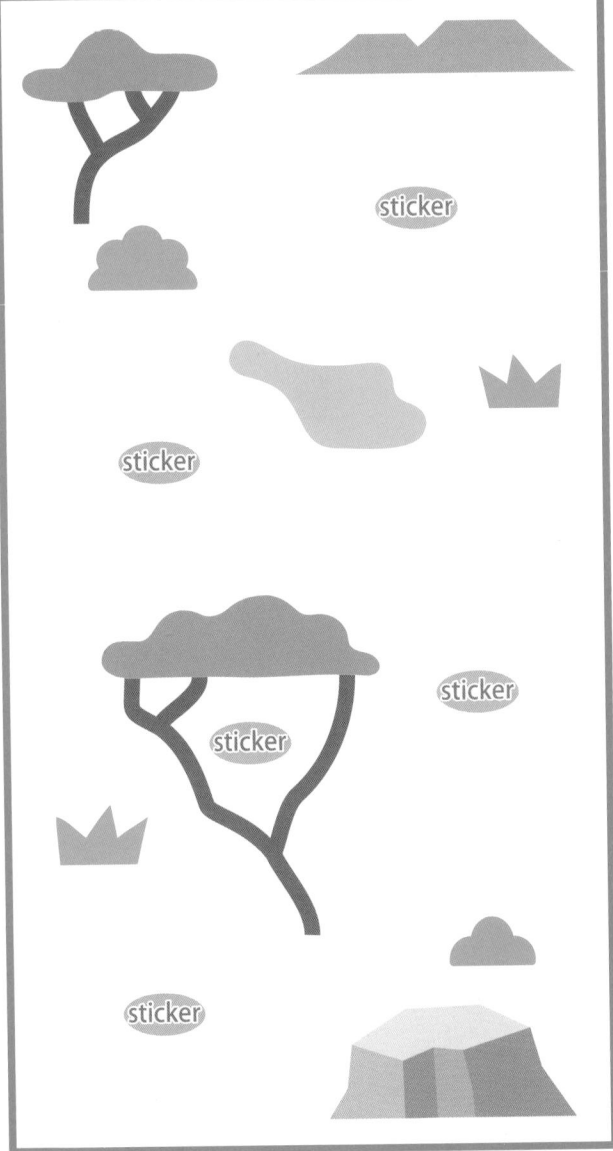

Animal Farm

Name the hiding animals. Then, put the matching animal sticker on the sticker next to it.

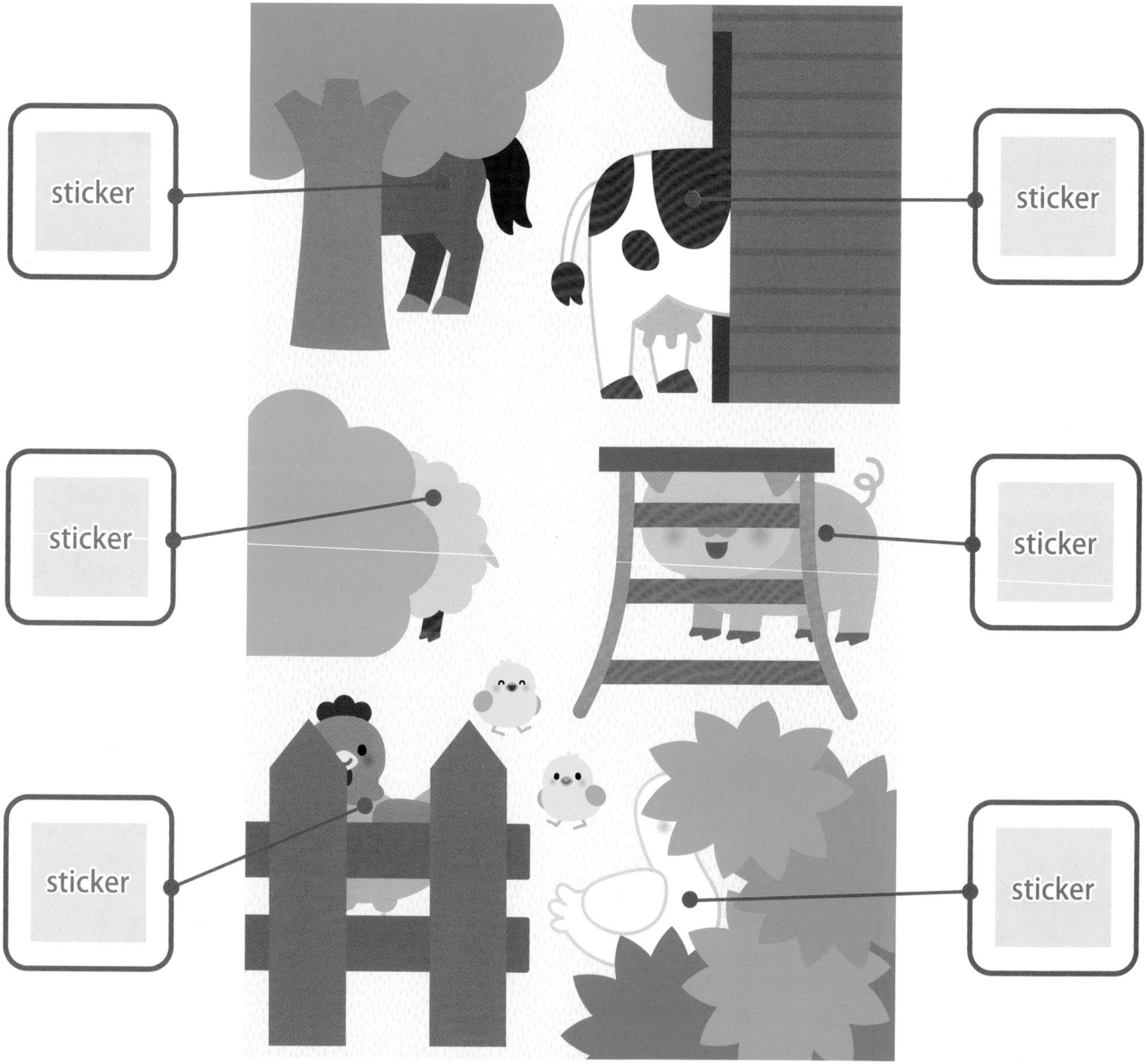

sticker

sticker

sticker

sticker

sticker

sticker

Sea Aquarium

Name the hiding sea creatures. Then, put the matching sea creature sticker on the [sticker] next to it.

sticker

sticker

sticker

sticker

sticker

sticker

Complete the Picture

Put a sticker on [sticker] to complete each picture.

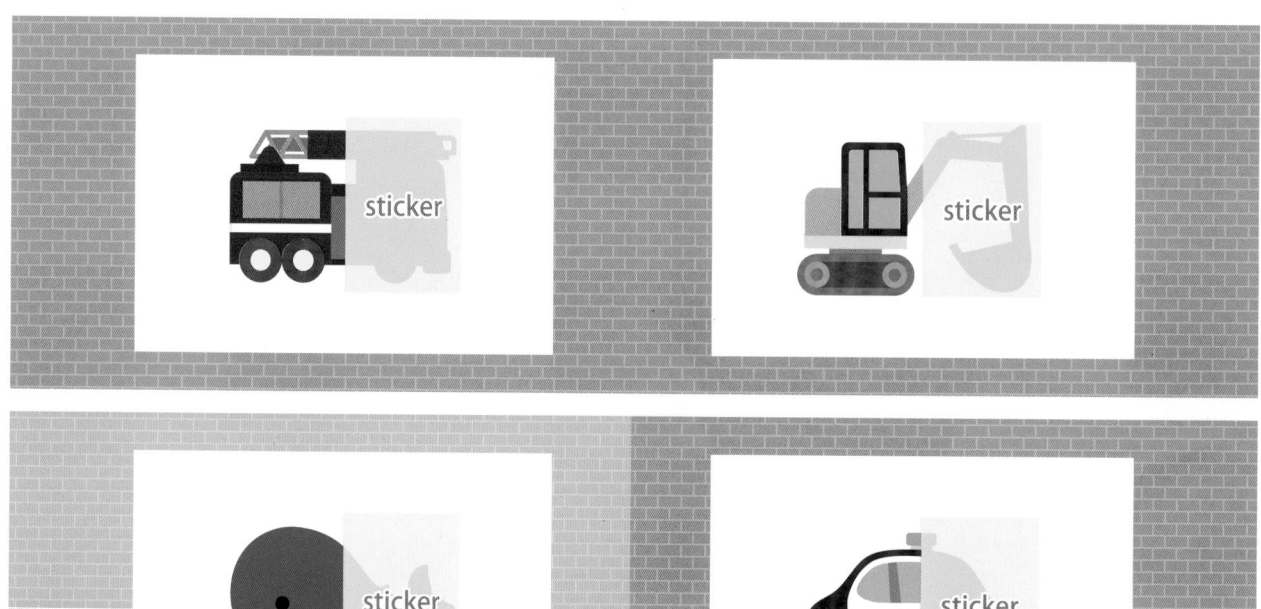

Creativity

Vegetable Friends

Add eyes, a mouth, and arms stickers to each vegetable.

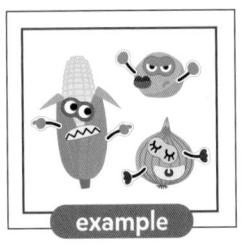

example

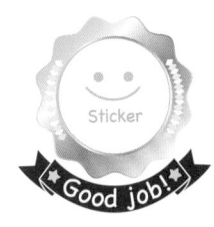

Sticker
Good job!

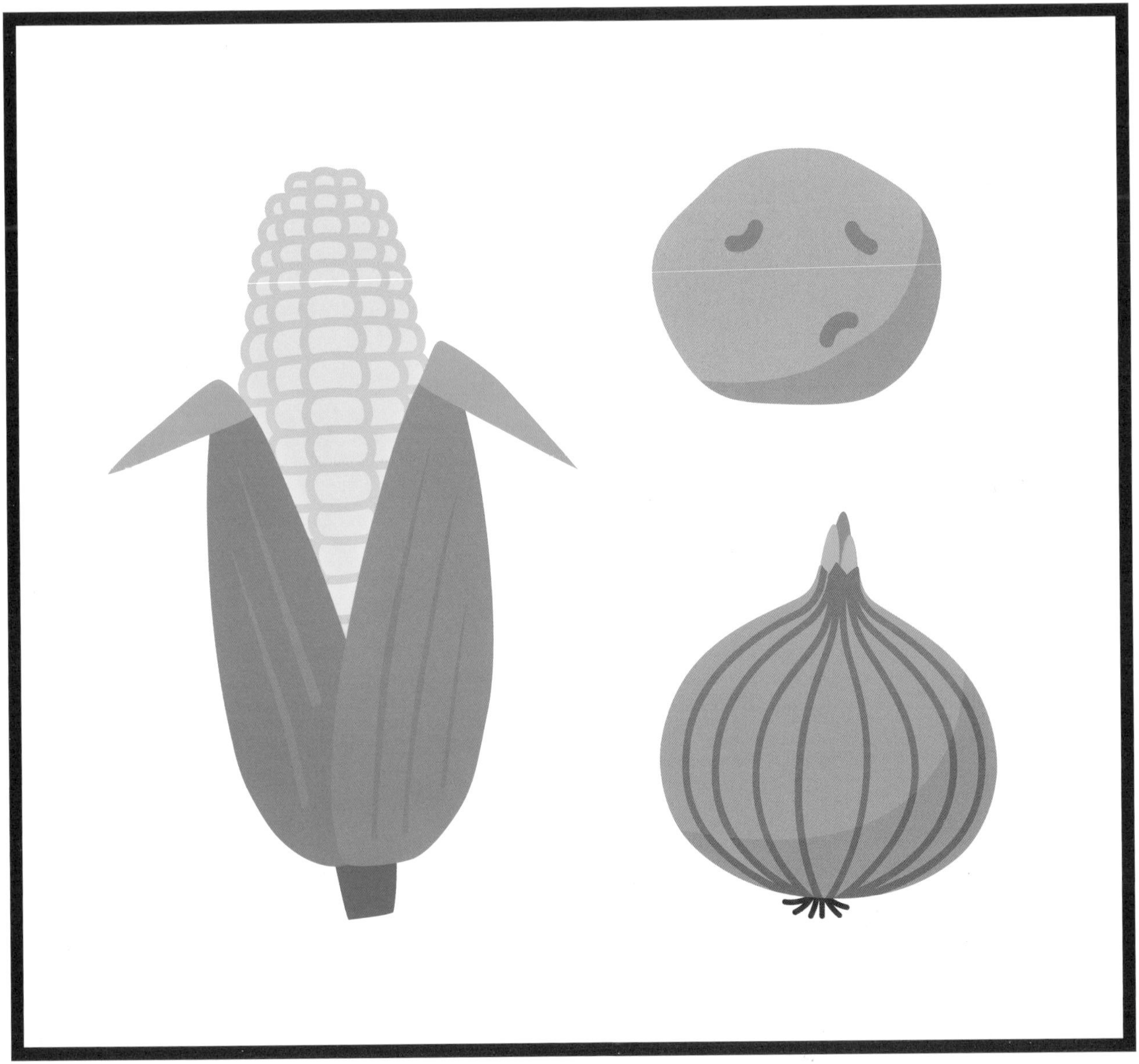

Hungry Cats

Put a bowl sticker in front of each cat.

Hats On

Put a hat sticker on each child.

Food Match

Put each sandwich sticker on the shape that matches its size. Then, put each hot dog sticker on the shape that matches its size.

Sticker

Good job!

sticker

sandwiches

sticker

sticker

hot dogs

sticker

Food Match

Put each apple pie sticker on the shape that matches it size. Then, put each cheeseburger sticker on the shape that matches its size.

sticker

sticker

sticker

apple pies

sticker

sticker

sticker

cheeseburgers

Glove Pairs

Find the sticker that matches each glove to make a pair.

sticker

sticker

sticker

sticker

sticker

Shoe Pairs

Find the sticker that matches each shoe to make a pair.

Good job!

sticker

sticker

sticker

sticker

sticker

19

Creativity

Make a Snowman

Complete the snowman by adding hat and scarf stickers.
Then, add more snowball stickers to the snowy scene.

example

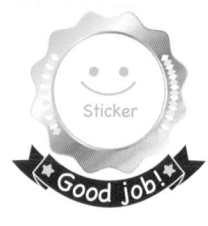

Sticker
Good job!

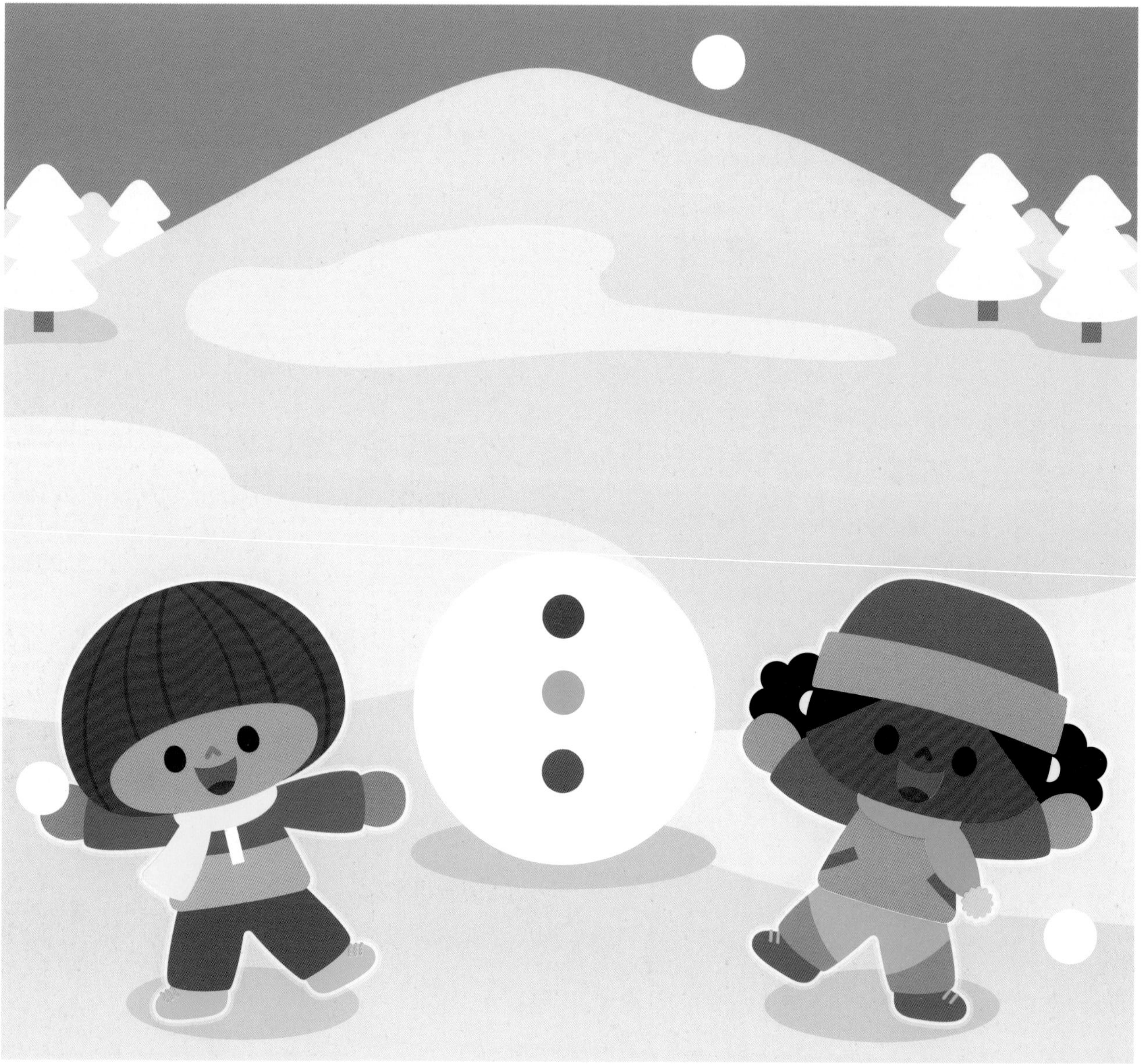

Creativity

Starry Sky

Put star stickers in the night sky. Then, add shooting star and moon stickers.

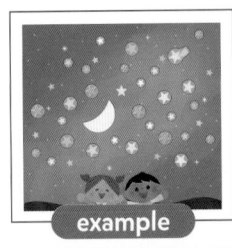

example

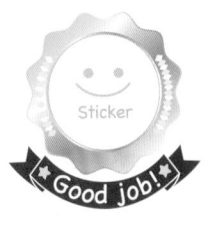

Sticker
Good job!

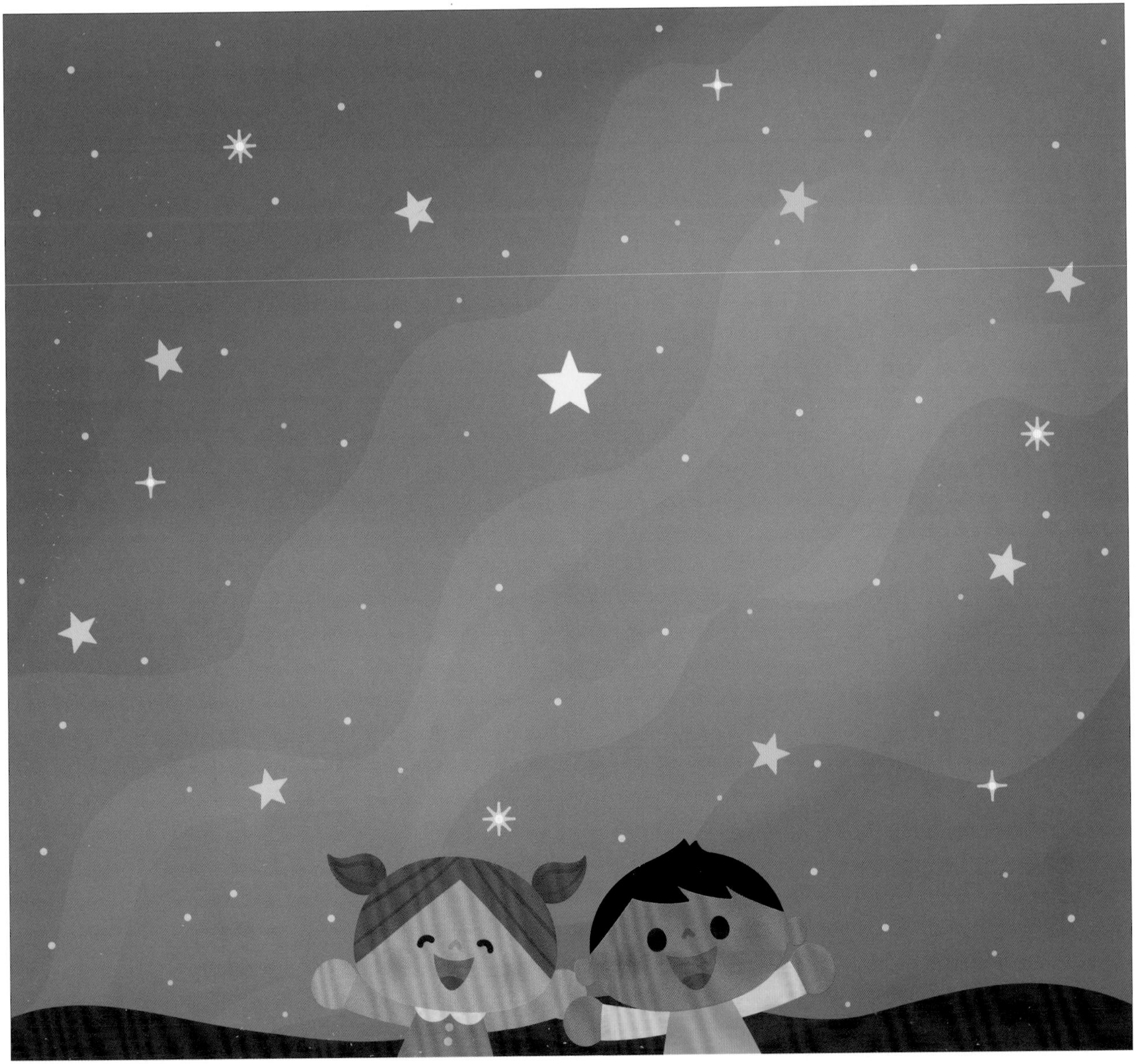

Things That Start with A

Say the name of each thing hiding behind the letter A. Then, put its matching sticker on the sticker .

Sticker
Good job!

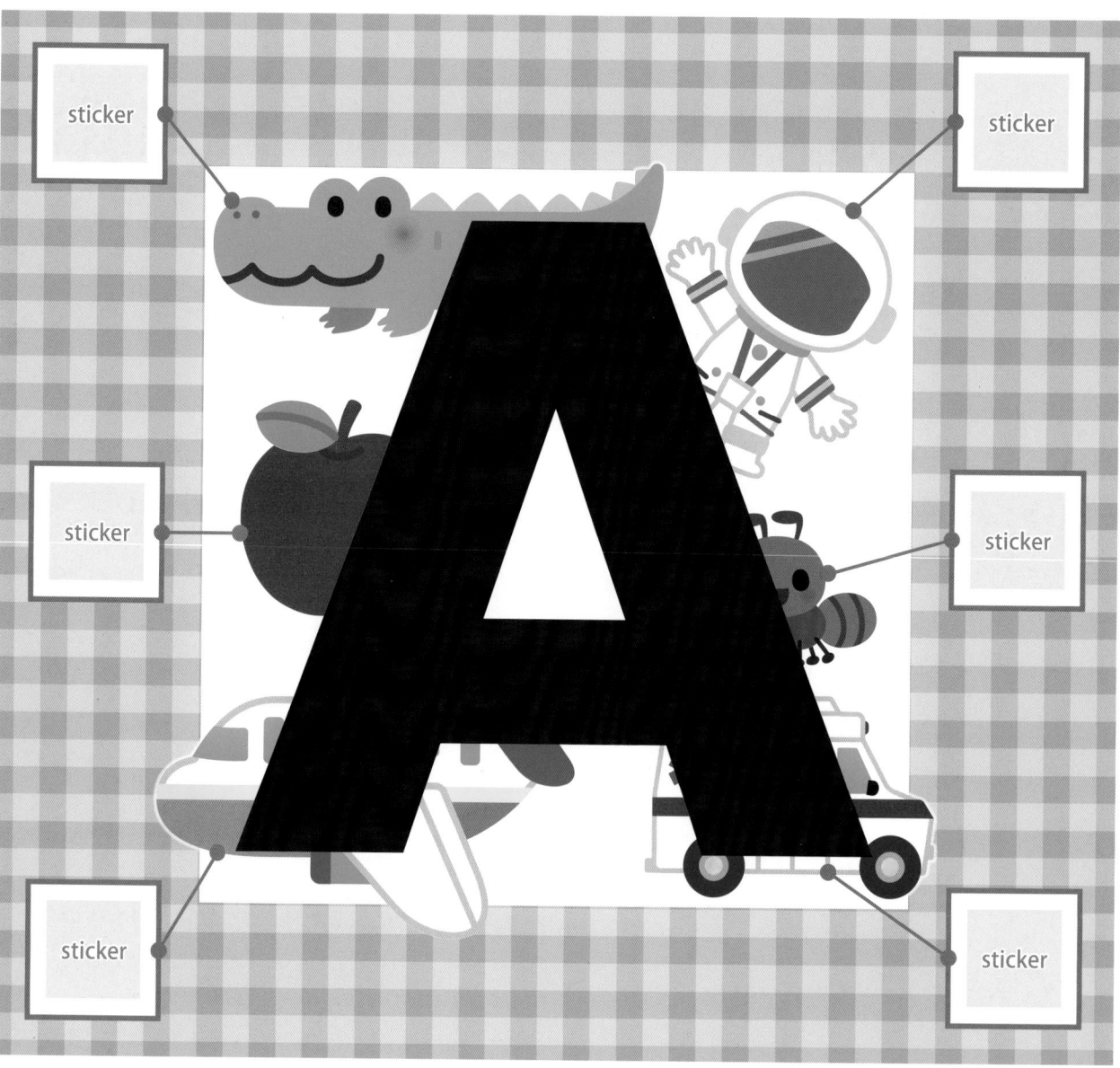

Things That Start with B

Say the name of each thing hiding behind the letter B. Then, put its matching sticker on the sticker .

sticker

sticker

sticker

sticker

sticker

sticker

ABC Maze

Follow the path in the order of the alphabet. As you go, put the letter stickers on the path. Then, put stickers on the matching sticker .

Sticker

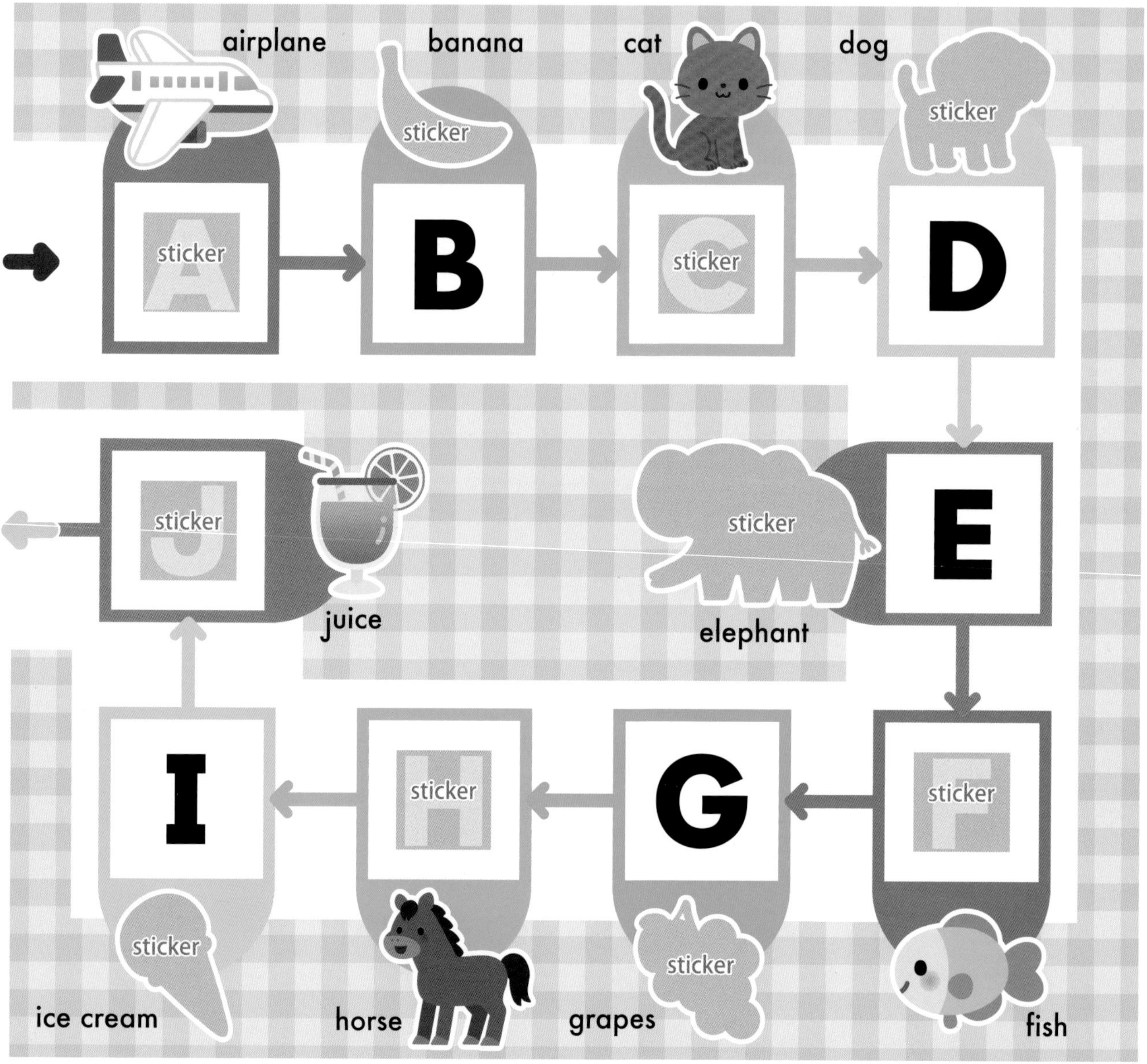

Good job!

airplane   banana   cat   dog

A   B   C   D

E

juice   elephant   F

I   H   G

ice cream   horse   grapes   fish

Numbers

Sweet Cookies

Add stickers so that each plate has 5 cookies.

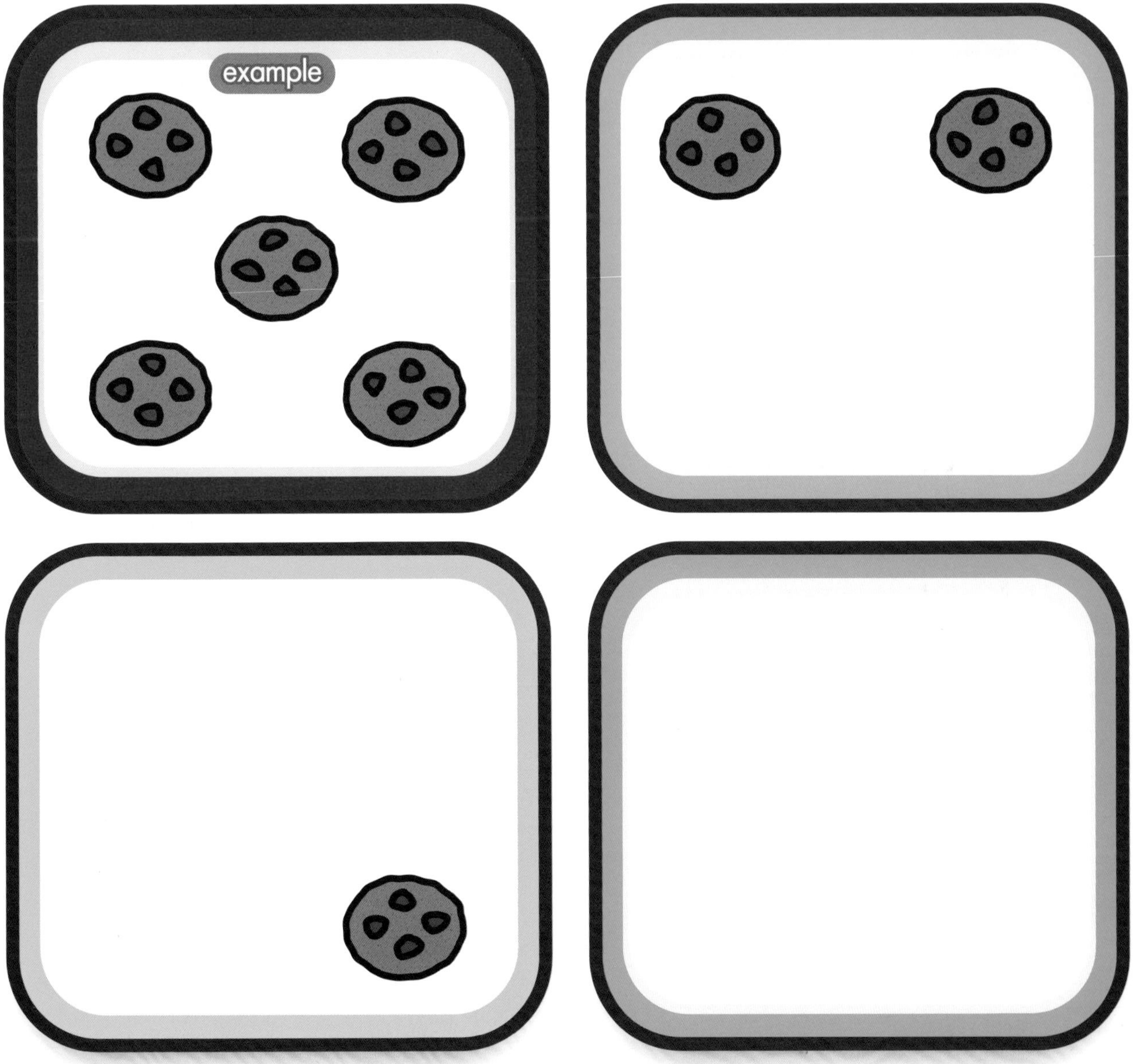

Counting Flowers

Count the flowers. Add the number sticker to the box that matches the number of flowers.

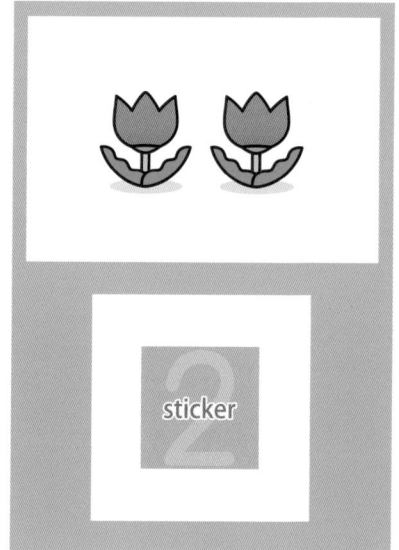

Counting Candy

Count the candy. Add the number sticker to the box that matches the number of candies.

sticker

sticker

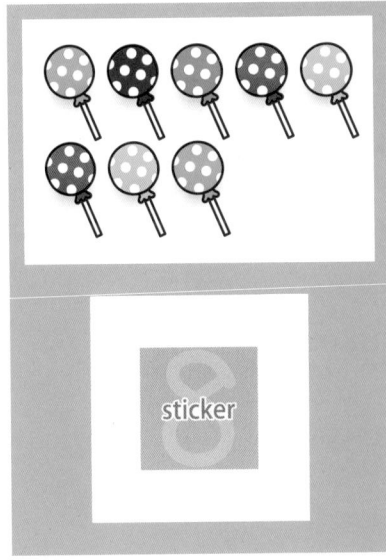

sticker

sticker

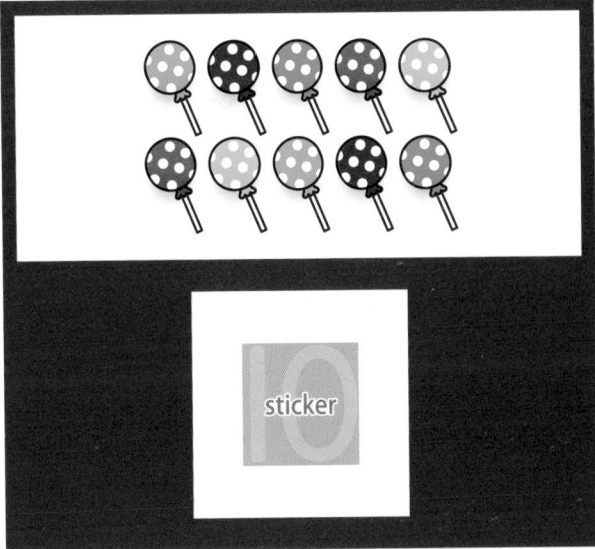

sticker

Number Maze

Follow the path from ➡ to ➡ in the order of smallest to largest. As you go, put number stickers on the path. When finished, count the number of fish.

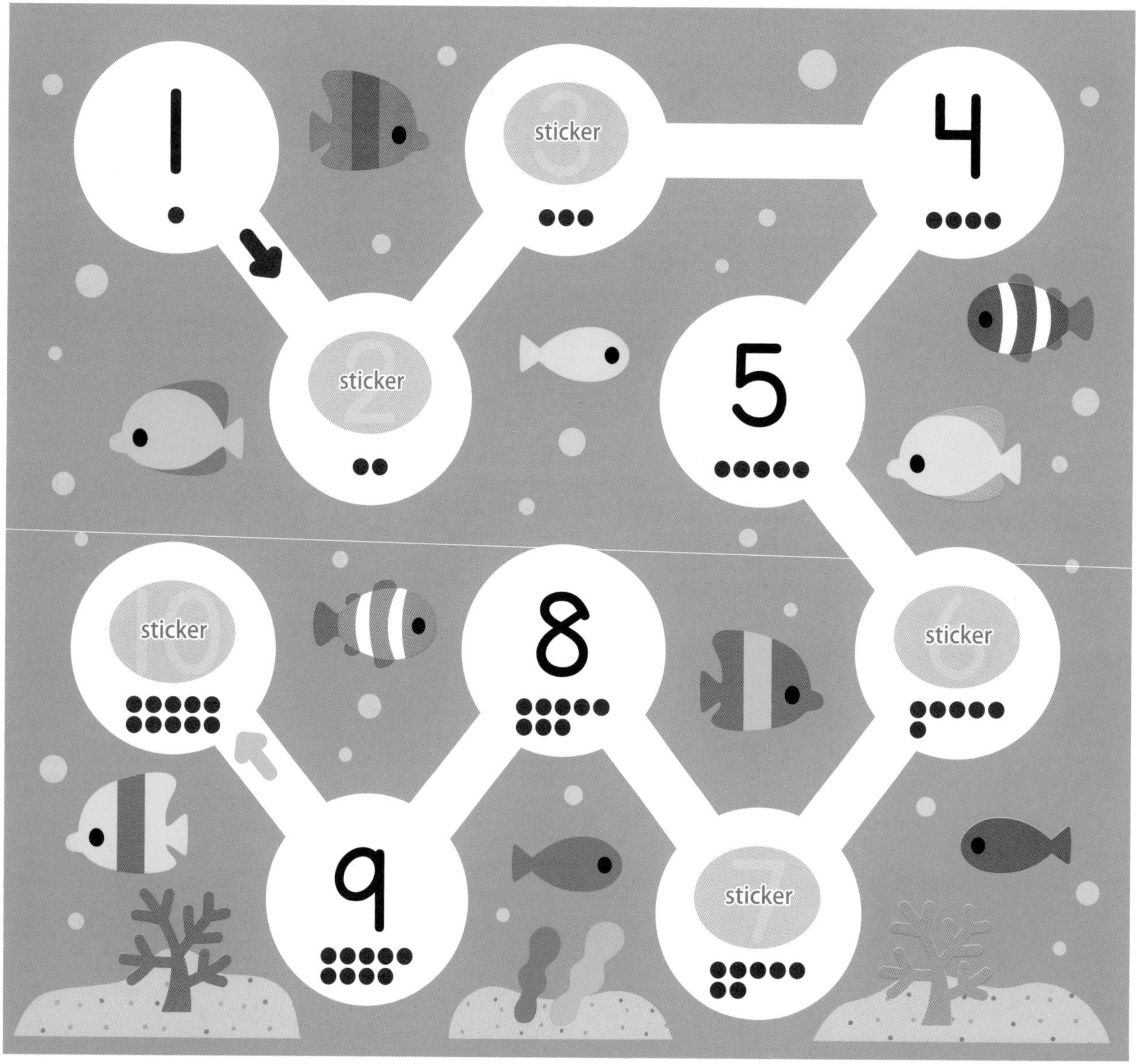

Good job!

Sticker

1

sticker •••

4 ••••

sticker ••

5 •••••

sticker •••••••••

8 •••••••••

sticker •••••

9 •••••

sticker •••••

Things That Go Together

Find the stickers that belong together. Then, put them in each color group.

Sticker

Good job!

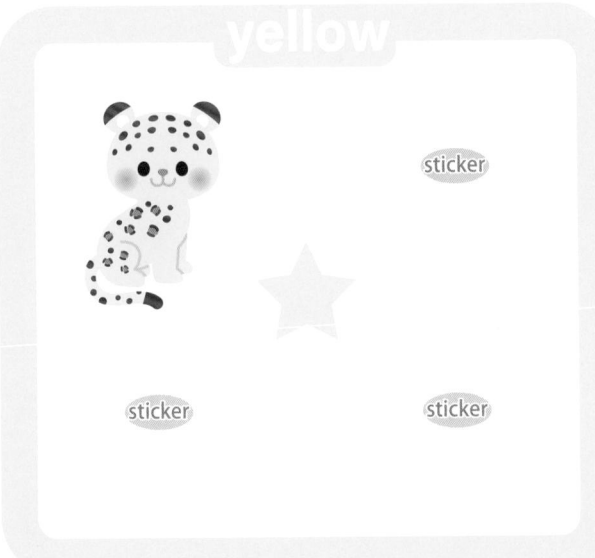

yellow

sticker

sticker

sticker

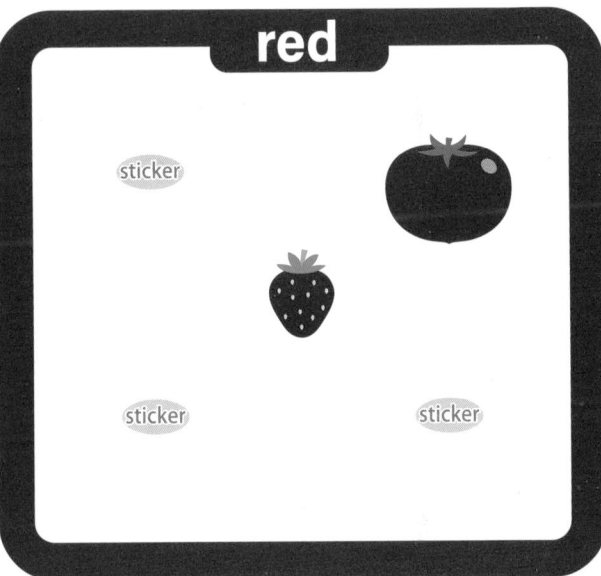

red

sticker

sticker

sticker

sticker

sticker

sticker

green

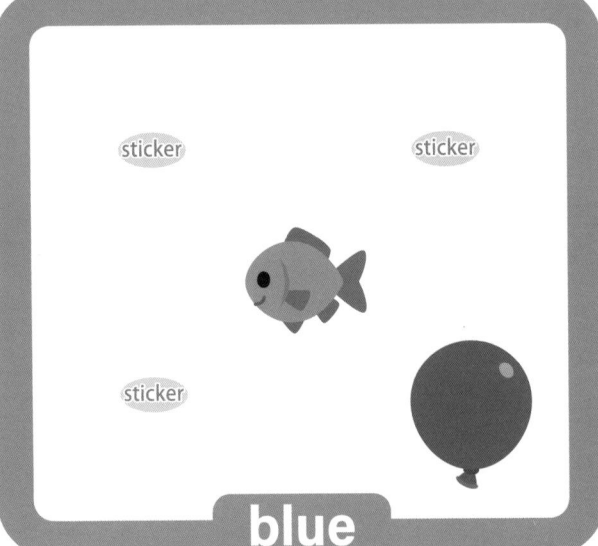

sticker

sticker

sticker

blue

Matching Game

Vehicle Parts

Guess the vehicle from its part. When you name the vehicle, put a sticker on its shadow.

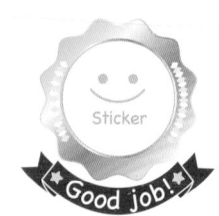

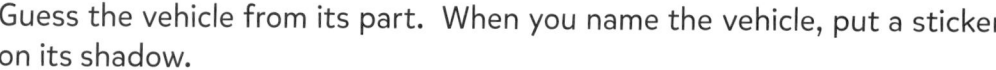

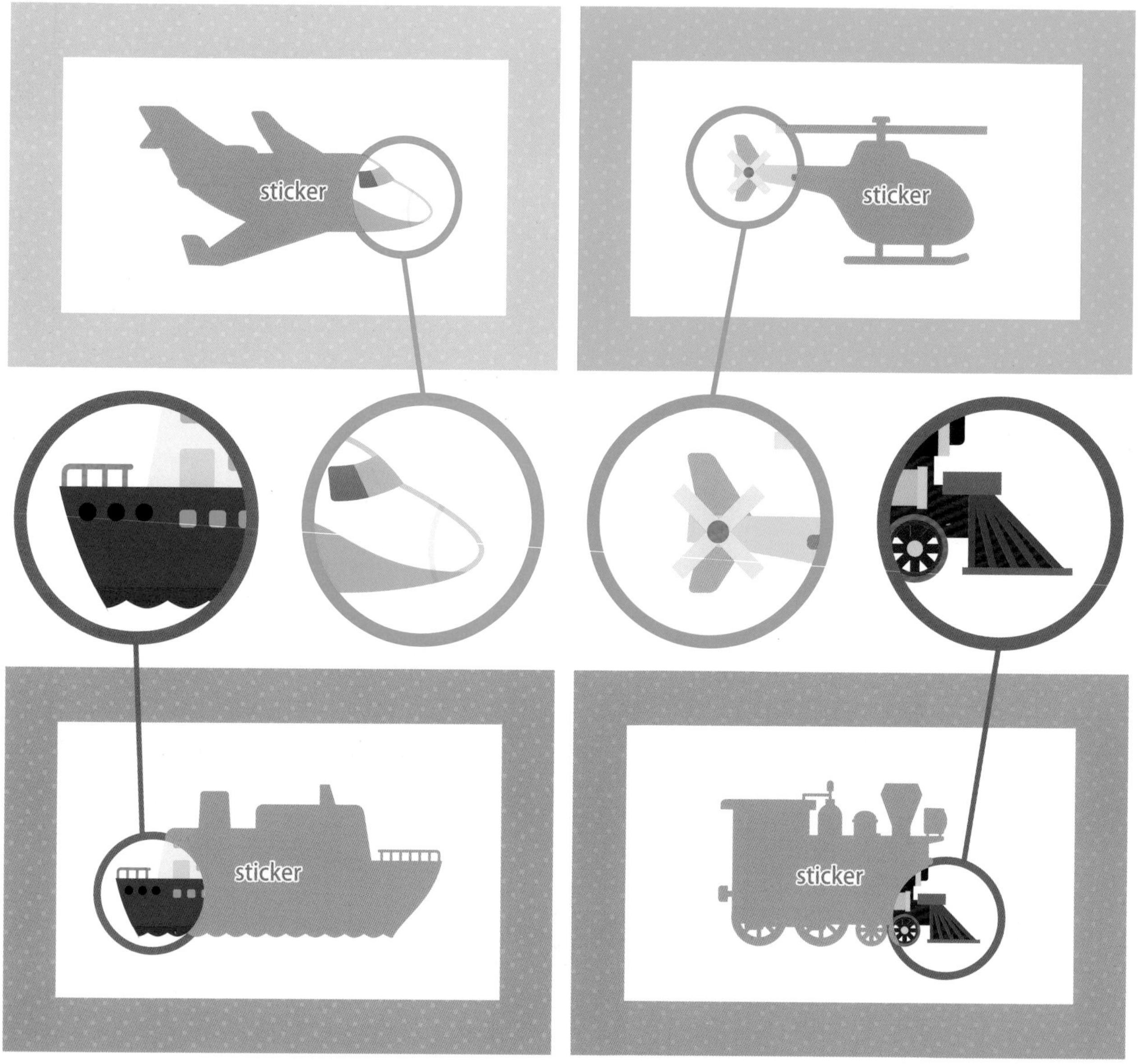

Matching Match

Each picture shows the front of an animal. Put a sticker next to the animal that shows it from the side.

sticker	sticker
sticker	sticker
sticker	sticker

Pattern Play

Follow the path from ➡ to ➡ while putting stickers on (sticker) in this order:

Pattern Play

Follow the path from ➡ to ⟱ while putting stickers on sticker in this order:

(sticker) (sticker) (sticker)

sticker

sticker

sticker

sticker

Pattern Puzzle

Sticker
Good job!

Follow the pattern in the example to create the same pattern in the boxes on the right.

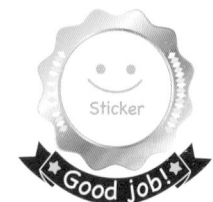

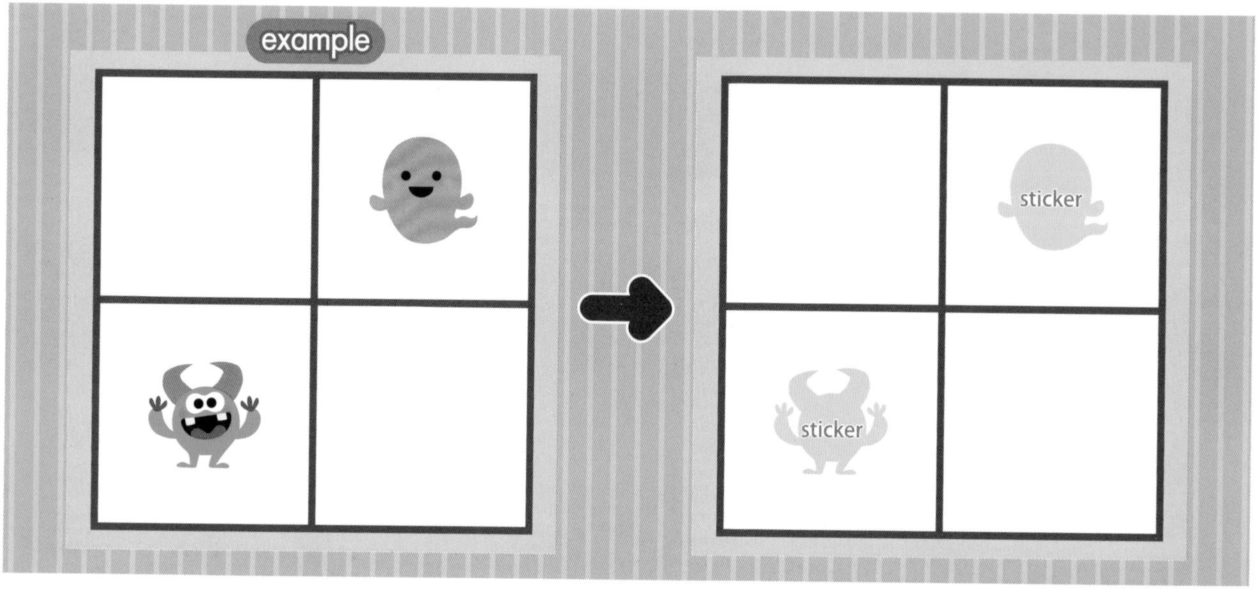
example
sticker
sticker

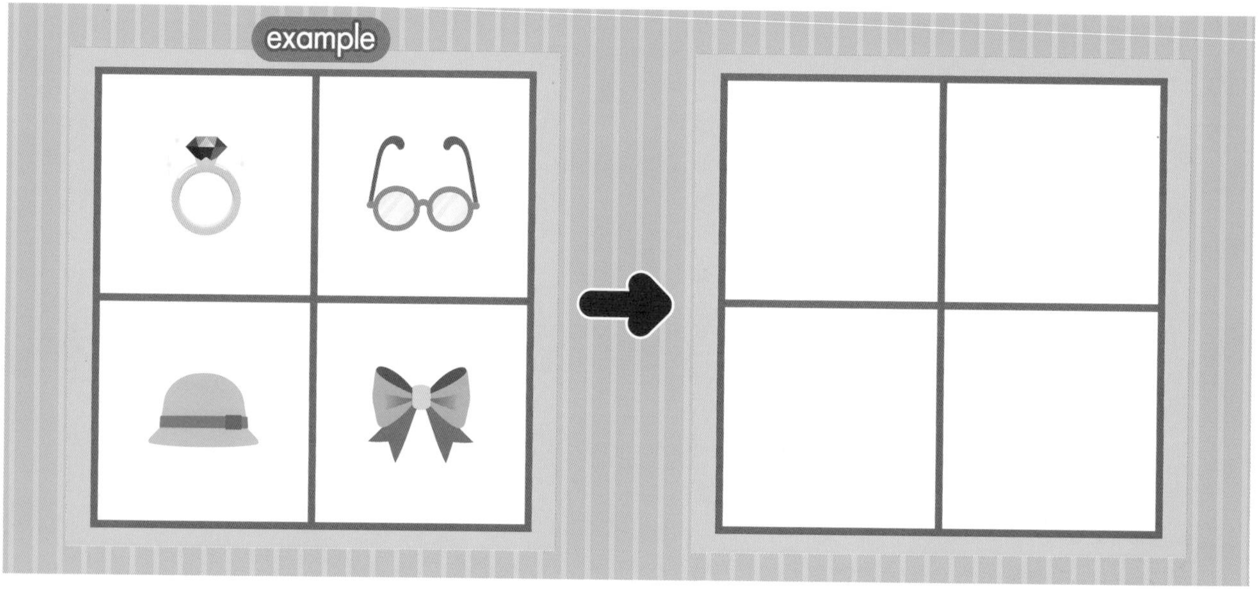
example

Pattern Puzzle

Follow the pattern in the example to create the same pattern in the boxes on the right.

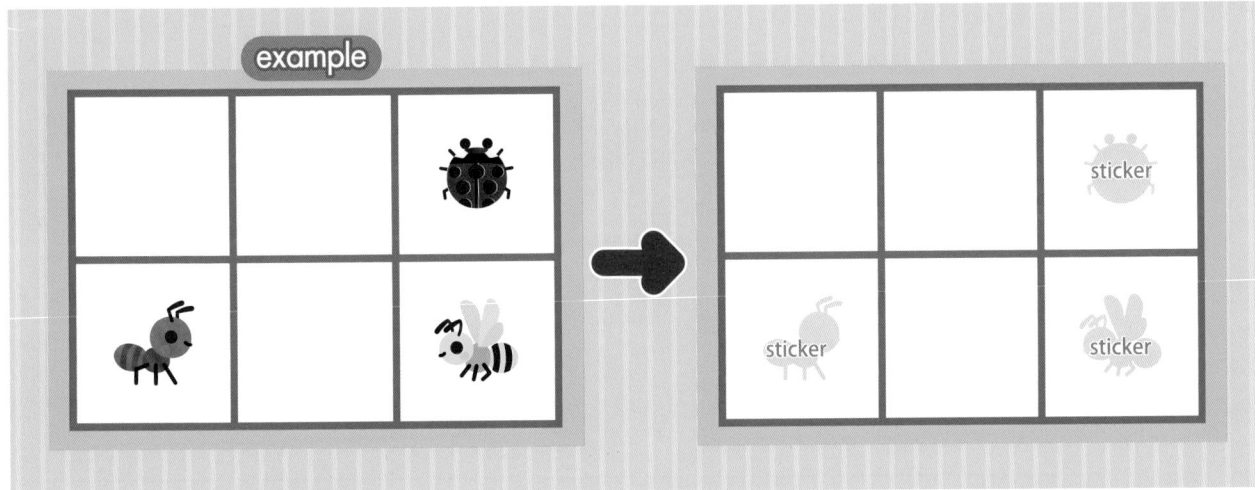

Numbers

Snack Time

Add stickers so each child's tray has a cheeseburger, a box of french fries, and a cup of juice.

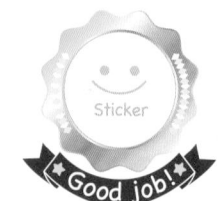

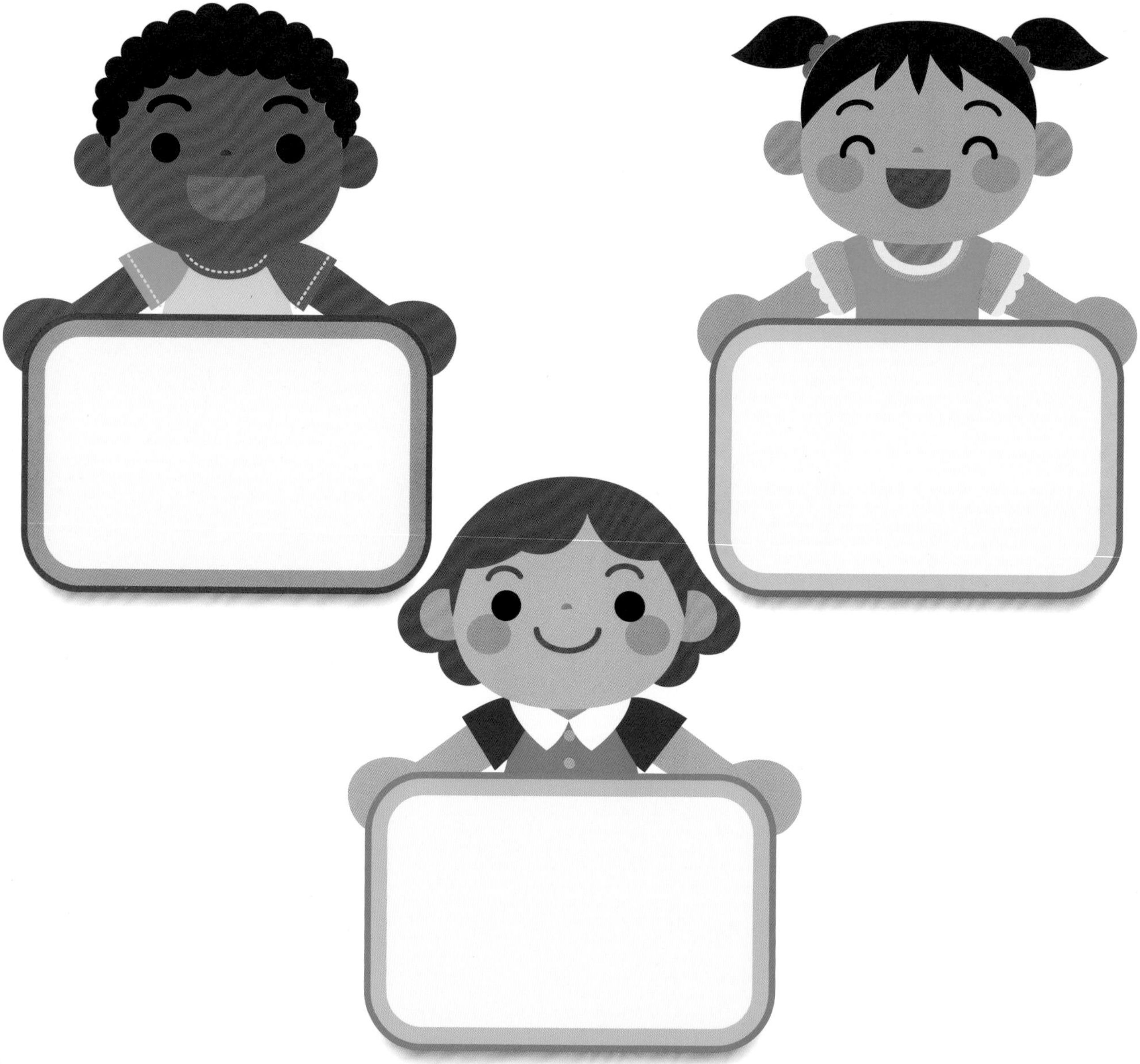

Fruit Maze

Follow the path from ➡ to ➡ while putting fruit stickers on their matching shadows.

Good job!
Sticker

sticker

sticker

sticker

sticker

sticker

sticker

37

Maze

Connect the Bridges

Connect the missing bridges with stickers. Then, follow the path from ➡ to ➡.

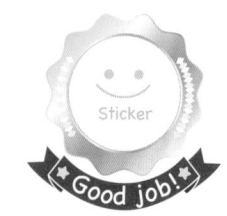

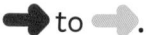

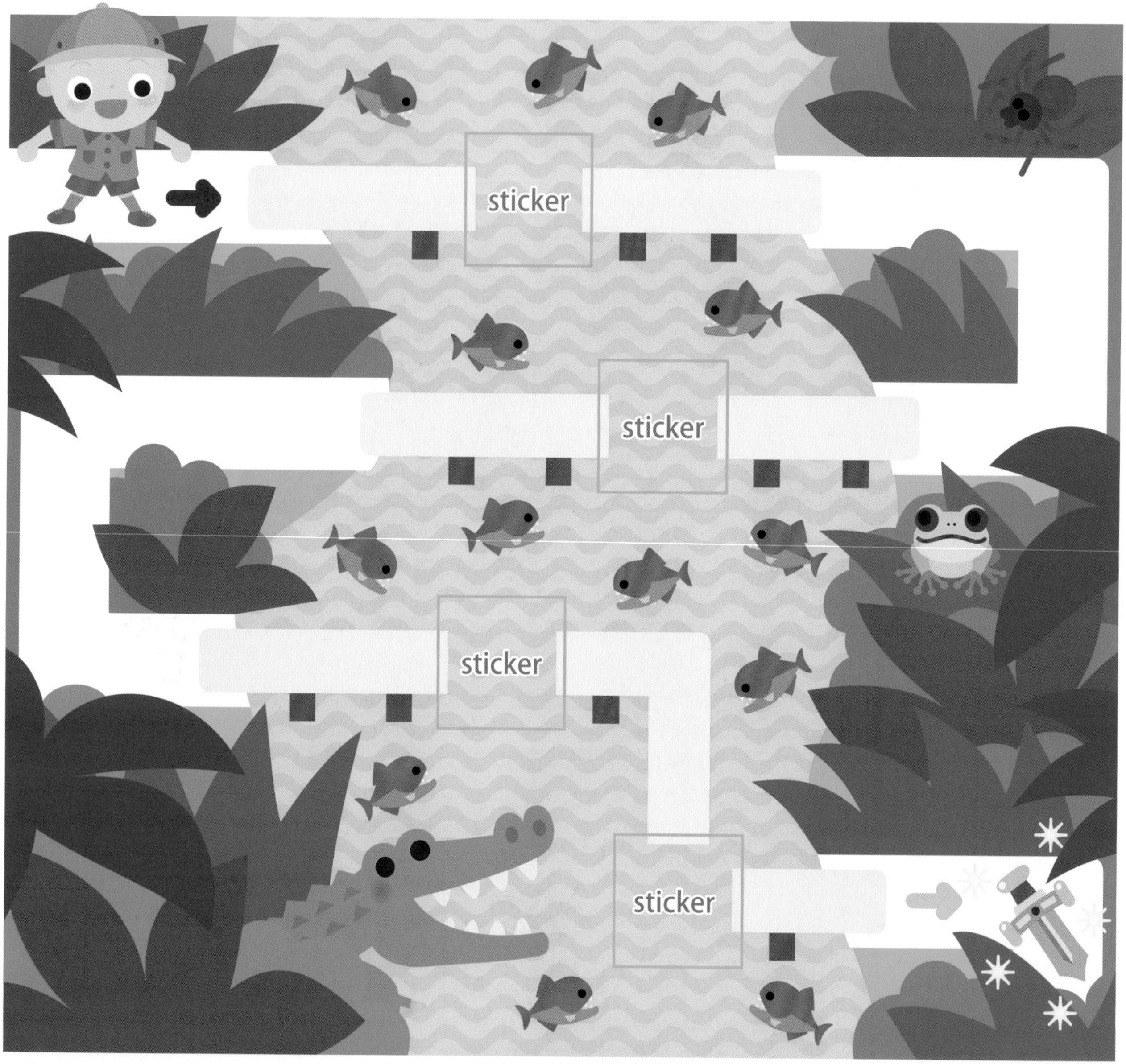

Maze

Fix the Road

Fix the broken road with stickers. Then, follow the path from ➡ to ➡.

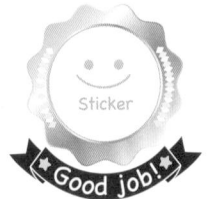

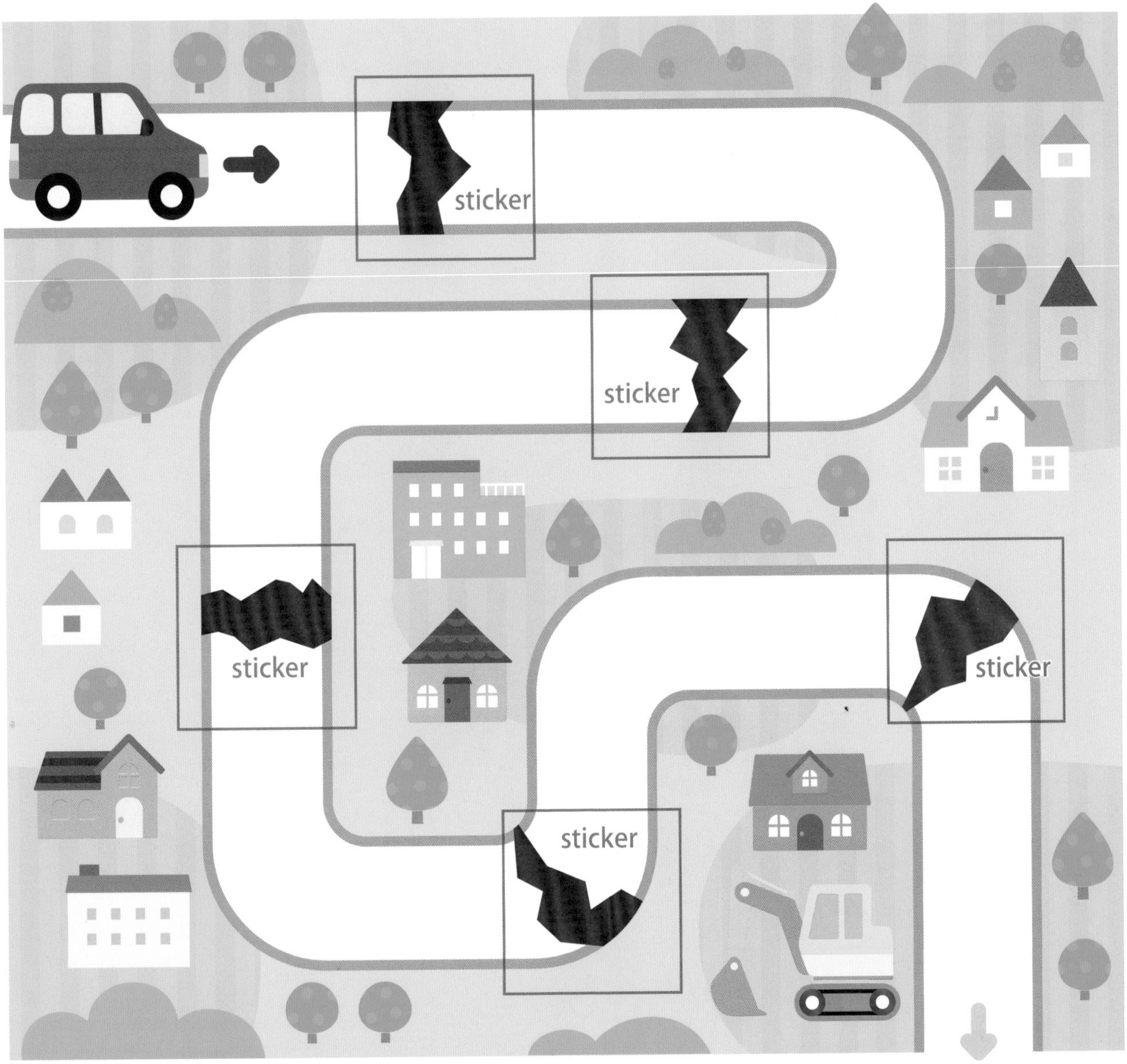

At the Amusement Park

Put ■▲♥★ stickers on their matching shapes to complete the scene.

Good job!

sticker

sticker

sticker

sticker

40

Creativity

Playground Games

Put playground stickers on the grass wherever you'd like. Then, add animal and flower stickers.

example

Sticker
Good job!

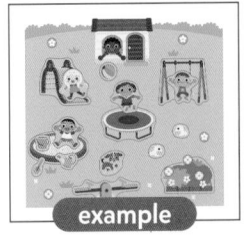

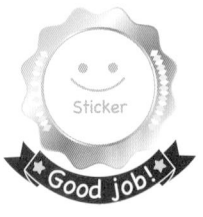

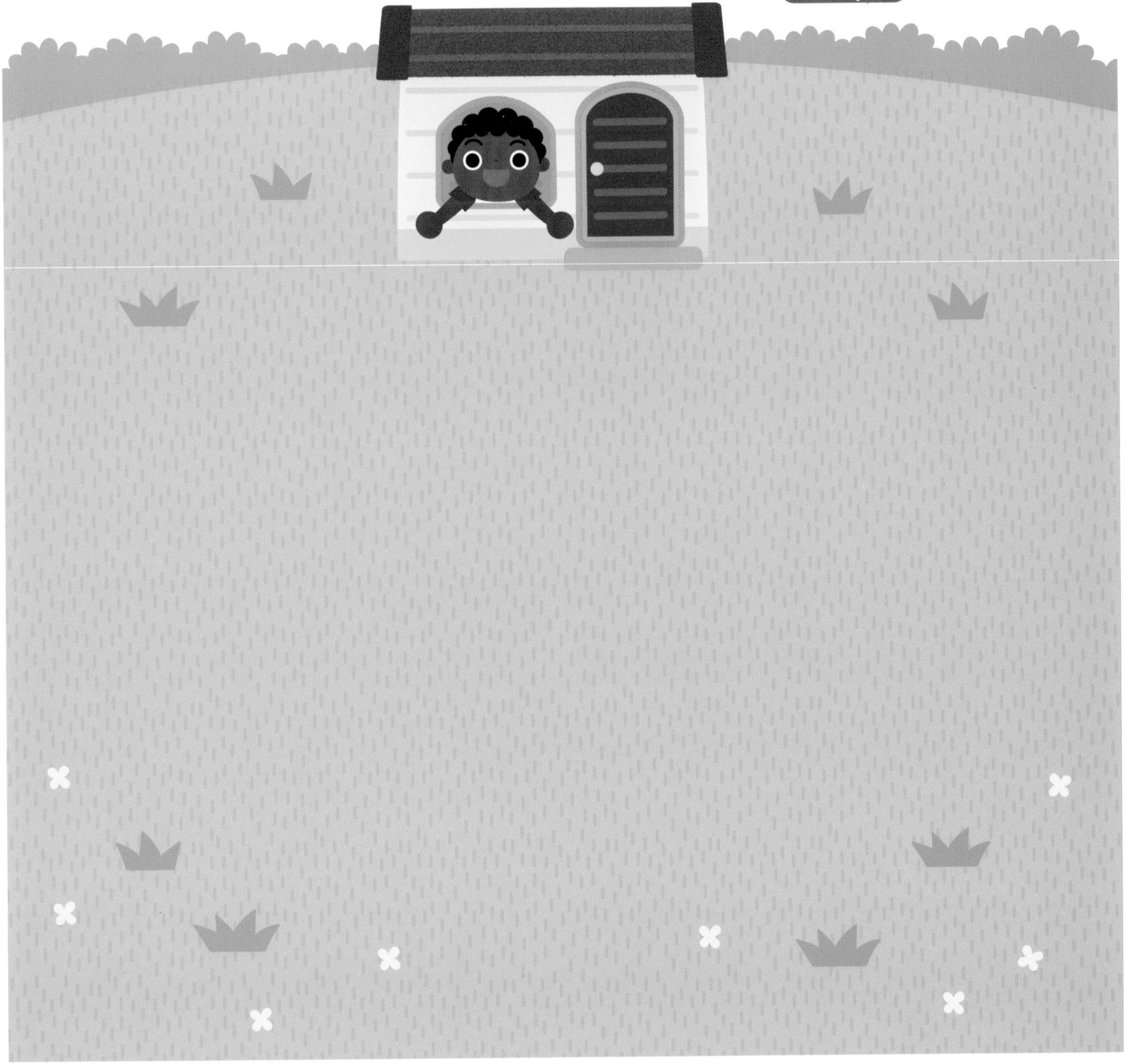

Classification

Playroom

Help keep the children's room tidy. Put the book and toy stickers on the correct shelf.

bookshelf
toy shelf
example

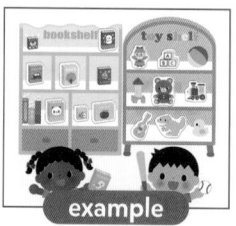

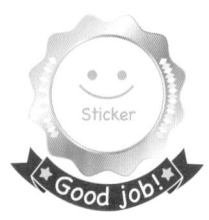

Sticker
Good job!

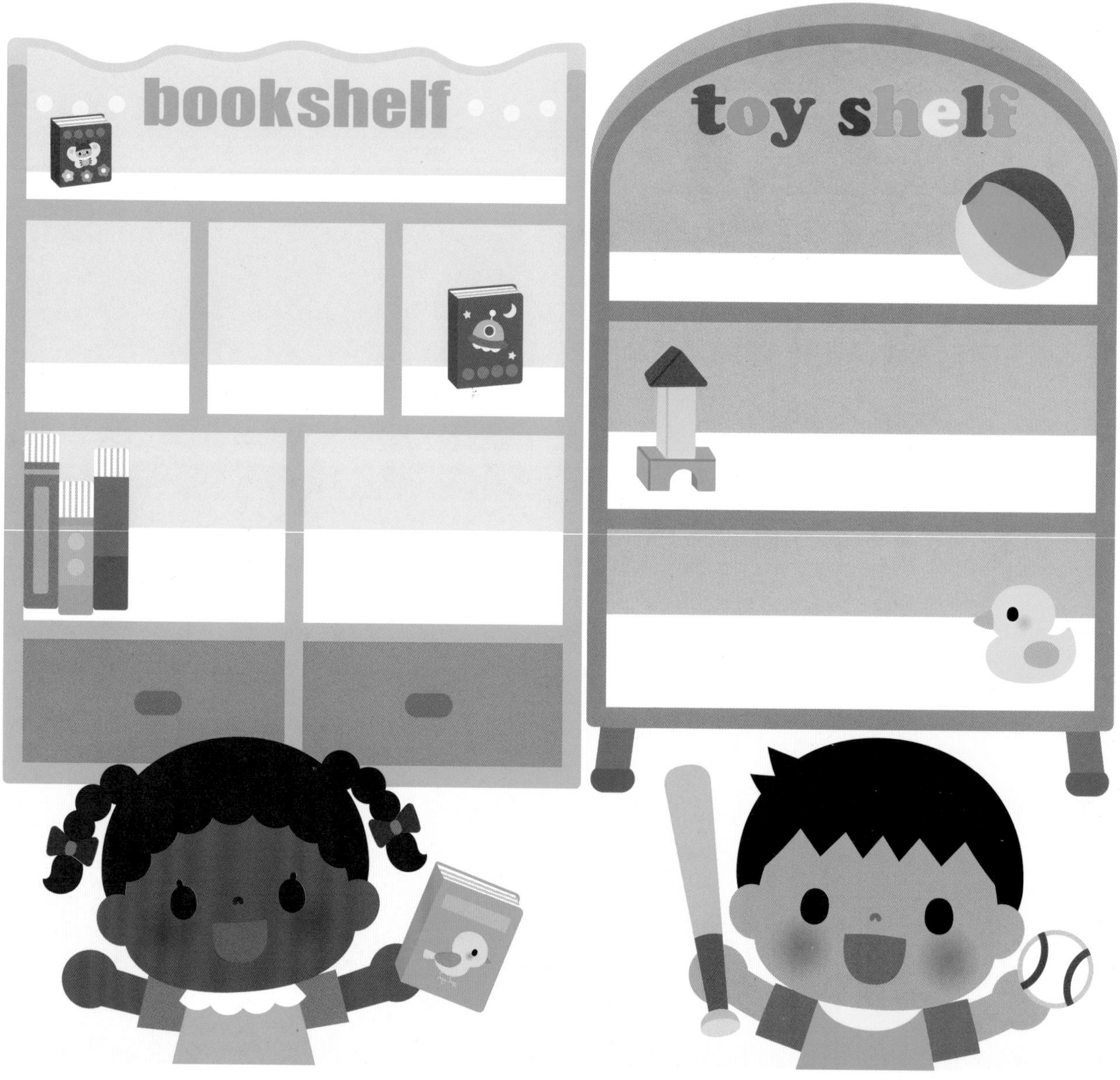
bookshelf
toy shelf

Nail Art

Decorate the nails with your favorite stickers.
Then, add the ring stickers.

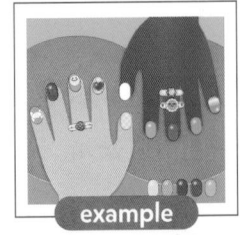

example

Sticker

Good job!

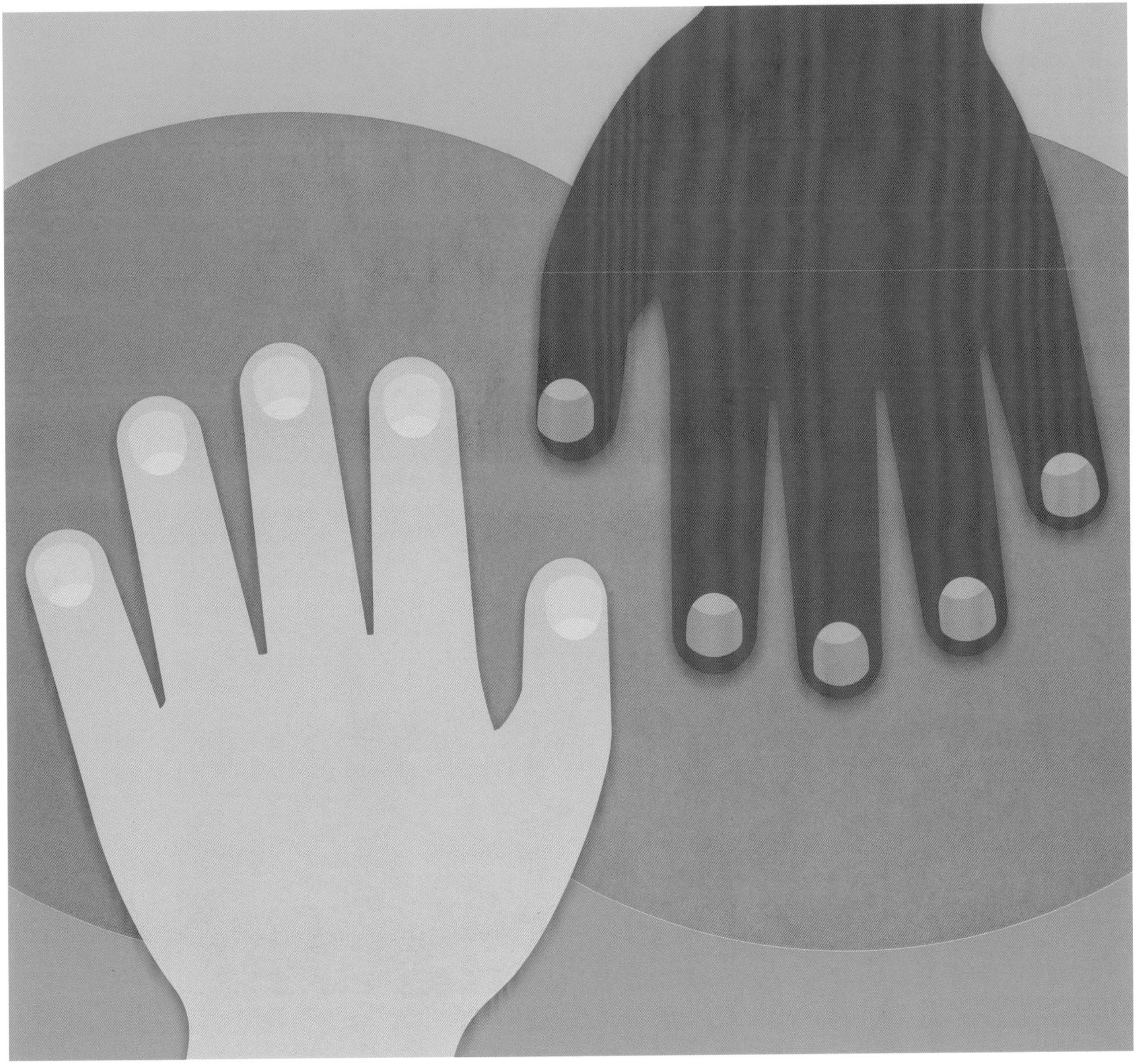

Decorate a Bag

Decorate the bag with your favorite stickers.

example

Sticker

Good job!

BAG

Creativity

Decorate a Dino T-Shirt

Decorate the T-shirt with your favorite stickers.

DINOSAUR
example

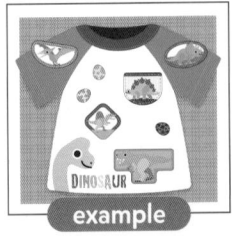

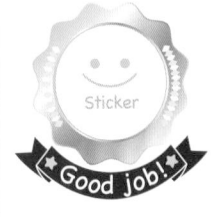

Sticker
Good job!

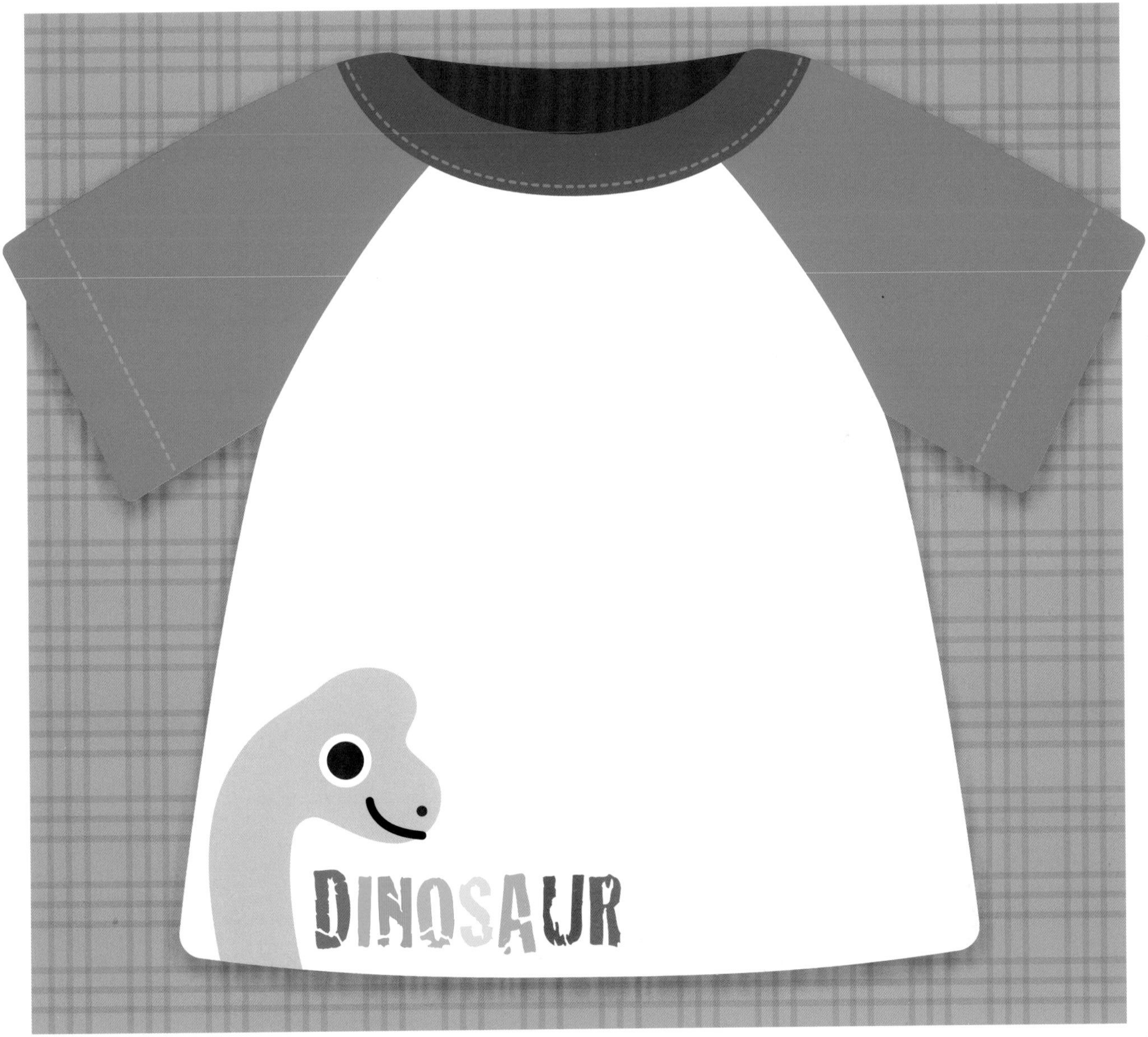
DINOSAUR

Creativity

Decorate the Outfit

Decorate the dress with stickers.

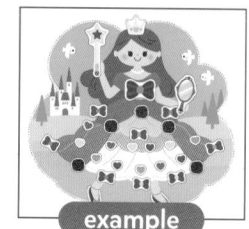

example

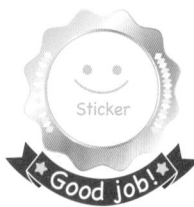

Sticker
Good job!

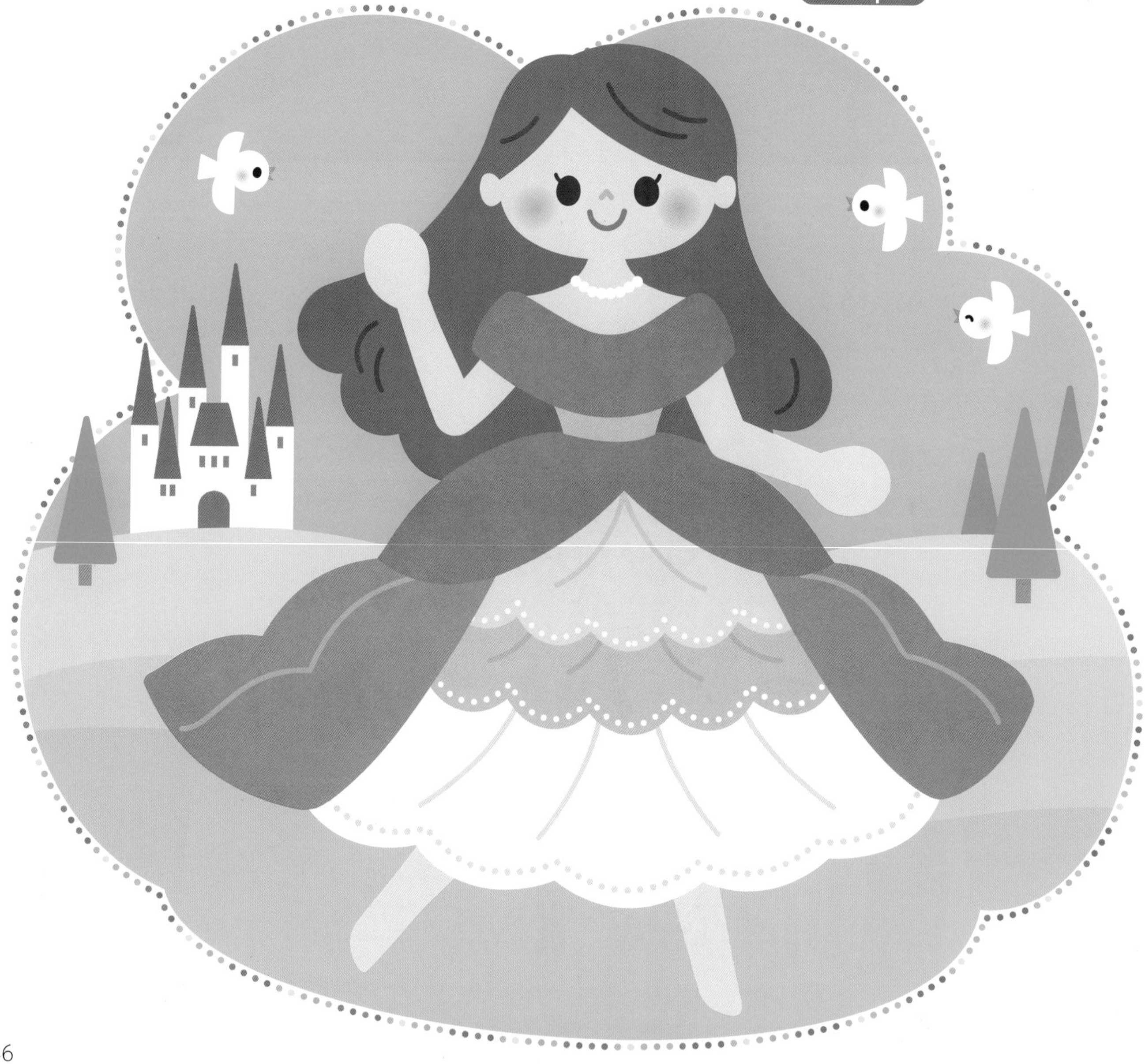

Castle Puzzle

Put stickers on the castle so they match the shapes.

example

Sticker

Good job!

sticker

sticker sticker

sticker sticker

sticker sticker

sticker sticker sticker

sticker sticker sticker sticker

sticker sticker sticker sticker

47

Globe Puzzle

Put stickers on the globe so they match the shapes and numbers.

Sticker
Good job!

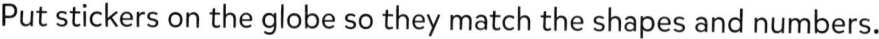